The Poodle Handbook

the
POODLE
HANDBOOK

by

Ernest H. Hart

with line drawings

and cover watercolor

by the author

Distributed in the U.S.A. by T.F.H. Publications, Inc., 211 West Sylvania Avenue, P.O. Box 27, Neptune City, N.J. 07753; in England by T.F.H. (Gt. Britain) Ltd., 13 Nutley Lane, Reigate, Surrey; in Canada to the book store and library trade by Clarke, Irwin & Company, Clarwin House, 791 St. Clair Avenue West, Toronto 10, Ontario; in Canada to the pet trade by Rolf C. Hagen Ltd., 3225 Sartelon Street, Montreal 382, Quebec; in Southeast Asia by Y.W. Ong, 9 Lorong 36 Geylang, Singapore 14; in Australia and the south Pacific by Pet Imports Pty. Ltd., P.O. Box 149, Brookvale 2100, N.S.W., Australia. Published by T.F.H. Publications, Inc. Ltd., The British Crown Colony of Hong Kong.

Cover drawing by Ernest H. Hart.

Frontispiece: Ch. Loramar's I'm A Dandee, owned by Mr. and Mrs. Robert D. Levy and bred by Loramar Kennels. Sire: Ch. Challendon Ivy League; dam: Loramar's Pixie. This brown Toy has established himself as a top winner among all three varieties in the breed. Always owner-handled, this great dog has been fearlessly campaigned from coast to coast and has met and beaten top competition in all parts of the United States. Photo by Evelyn Shafer.

ISBN 0-87666-359-5

Contents

To my youngest son, Keith,
who knows the value of
a Poodle's companionship.

Foreword

To write a book, any book, is not an easy task. But writing and illustrating is my job, my vocation, and dogs are my hobby, so a marriage of the two would seem to be a desired accomplishment. This book, and others of like category, are the inevitable issue of the above union.

With each book of this kind that I write an amazing amount of data must be accumulated, assessed, sifted through, and selected from, followed by weeks of study and critical appraisal to separate the wheat from the chaff and true fact from mere opinion. This is the lot of the writer in a specialty field such as this, to immerse oneself in dry research, to dig and dig and dig some more until there is nothing left to find and then to objectively assemble all that is worthwhile into literary form.

It is a job almost, of reporting, but with this vital difference; I do not feel that I can make any statement without proving it correct, and answering the many questions, projected of course by myself, that I feel you would ask.

I have attempted to anticipate your every need, your every query in regard to this, the breed of your choice, and to present the answers in a fashion which you will understand and, I hope, enjoy reading. I hope that, with this book, I have made a positive contribution to the meagre and often controversial literature dedicated to the Poodle. I know that some of you will disagree with certain precepts and concepts within these covers that run contrary to your own experience and belief. That is as it should be, for no man is perfect, no book written by man is ever the complete and end answer, and intelligent argument is ever the basis for new thought, theory, and improvement.

To those of you who have graciously allowed the use of requested photographs of particular dogs, we (the publisher and I) offer thanks. Thanks also, to my son, Dr. Allan H. Hart, for his help in the chapter on diseases and first aid. My thanks, too, to my wife, Kay, whose silent encouragement helped to keep me on schedule and always acts as a spur to creative thought. And last but by no means least, thanks to all those learned people listed in the bibliography (present company excepted) from whom I have selected and borrowed the results of years of research and knowledge, to give to you.

No, writing this book has not been an easy task, but I am sure that neither has it been a fruitless one. I have learned much in its writing, and I sincerely hope that you will learn much in its reading.

ERNEST H. HART

Torremolinos, Spain

The Poodle Handbook

Ch. Blakeen Osprey, owned by Mrs. Sherman Hoyt. This white Standard was a well-known winner in the forties. Since that day the
Poodle has made a metéoric rise in popularity both as a show dog
and pet. Today Poodles can be found in most countries of the world.
Acme Photo.

Chapter 1
History of the Poodle

Canis familiaris aquatius; the Pudel or "water dog" of Germany, the name actually derived from the low German verb Puddelen, "to splash in water"; Caniche and Chiencanne in France, the names respectively meaning, "little duck" and "duck dog"; these were the labels by which a great breed was identified, a breed that in England was called the Poodle, the name which we in America adopted and use today.

Every breed of dog necessarily has its geneological background usually, and despite the claims of over enthusiastic fanciers, vanishing in the mists of careless time or merging with the history of other breeds. A few of the canine races are of recent enough vintage to be easily traced to their genetic sources, but the Poodle is not one of these. To find the ancestral elements from which the Poodle eventually emerged as a type or breed one must delve deeply into the past bringing to this research the added theory and accumulated data of a genetic detective.

Our first paragraph tells us definitely that in Germany and France the breed we call the Poodle was strongly associated with water and in the same sense as a modern day retriever is linked with this liquid element. The Poodle known and bred at the same early date in Russia was also recognized as a dog who would, indeed preferred, to work in water. The Poodle then, is closely allied to those breeds we know as sporting dogs, particularly those gundogs that retrieve in water.

The earliest known prototype dog, *Tomarctus*, who lived about 15 million years ago, was the ancestor of, among other canine species (foxes, jackals, wolves) four basic prehistoric types of Canis familiaris. The geneology of all breeds of dogs trace back to one or more of this pristine quartet. With two of them we have no concern, and to a third, *Canis familiaris inostranzewi*, we owe some small debt. But the fourth of these archtype breeds, *Canis familiaris intermedius* started the gene-pool from which the Poodle subsequently evolved.

Through the hoary eras of prehistory various mutations occurred in the chromosomes of the canine species. If these mutations favored the habitat of the animal, if they gave it a better pattern of survival or helped to better fit it to a new or changed environment then, through natural selection, the mutant survived while others of its kind died out. This, in all species of living things, is Charles Darwin's "survival of the fittest." So the dog changed in ability and appearance in various parts of the world. Then man stepped up onto the stage of history, hairy, half erect, brutal and furtive, and the dog that he adopted, or that adopted him, over 100,000 years ago, was no more like the dog of today than that sub-human man resembled the modern model of homo sapiens.

Poodles are bred in three size varieties; Toy, Miniature, and Standard. All have the typical Poodle temperament and all adjust perfectly to any home and environment. Photo by Louise Van der Meid.

Ch. Puttencove Privateer, owned by Puttencove Kennels and bred by the owner and Kathleen Baker. Sire: Ch. Chantilly Lover Boy; dam: Ch. Puttencove Diantha. Photo by Evelyn Shafer.

Crude and mentally sluggish, our early ancestors yet had sense enough to use the dog eventually for hunting and guarding and later for various other tasks that came into being as man left savagery and graduated to greater wisdom and a more complicated way of life. Turning to the dog for aid, man then took the place of nature and began selecting for certain traits that would make his canine companion capable of accomplishing a greater variety of tasks. Correlations between mental aptitudes and physical aspects were noticed by man and, by selecting for these wanted traits, he modified and gradually molded the dog into distinct breeds which were better able to do specific jobs.

From the prototype canine, intermedius, man shaped the breeds that became the early spaniels and these breeds came into focus eventually in Spain and Portugal. These were the initial sporting dogs from which came a host of gundog breeds. The Poodle and the

Ch. Silver Swank of Sassafras, owned by Mrs. Pamela A. P. Ingram.
Photo by Evelyn Shafer.

Harmo Black Magnet, owned by Harmo Kennels.
Photo by Evelyn Shafer.

Irish Water Spaniel, breeds that are closely and geneologically associated, came from these ancient spaniels and later animals known as "water dogs."

These latter, curly-coated, retrieving Old English water dogs probably owed some of their aquatic ability to an early cross to a breed similar to the St. John's Newfoundland. This Newfoundland dog was smaller and lighter than the breed as we know it today. The Old English Water Spaniel was also the progenitor of what Dalziel, author of *British Dogs* (1881), called the Tweed Water Spaniel. The Old English water dog, or spaniel, was duplicated in several countries other than England at approximately the same time. Strong, willing, intelligent and with an inherited hunting and retrieving instinct, these "Water Dogges" were used for retrieving from the 15th to the 18th centuries and were undoubtedly the direct progenitor of the Poodle.

This charting of the Poodle's family tree brings to light several extremely interesting facts about the breed. One is that the New-

Ch. Lorac's Magic Gay Blade, owned by Mrs. Carol Josephson.
Photo by Evelyn Shafer.

foundland cross brought into the breed the genetic material of the prototype dog Canis familiaris inostranzewi from which stemmed the Mastiff type breeds. This accounts for the huge and massive Poodles that appeared in Russia during the 18th century and earlier that weighed over 80 pounds. This inostranzewi strain was also the progenitor of the *Gross* (great) and *Schaf* (sheep) Pudels of Germany. When the breed was in its formative state or just emerging into true type, it was of the large or standard size. The smaller sizes came later through selection and, in the case of the toy, the introduction of outcross breeding for small size.

Schaf, or sheepherding Pudels can still be seen near Garmisch-Partinkerchen in the shadow of the snow-capped Zugspitz in southern Germany. They are large, solid, heavy-boned animals. The same type of Poodle can be found in Switzerland, near Brienz, pulling carts filled with cans of milk. I have hunted behind a pair of smaller, but still coarse and heavy-boned black Poodles in Spain, whose ancestors, I was told, came from Germany. In Frankfurt, Germany,

A group of Poodles and their costumed owners at a dog show in Zürich, Switzerland. There are a number of marked differences in the manner of trimming and the correct size in these dogs as compared to show Poodles in the United States.

I was shown a brace of native Pudels used as sporting dogs. All these animals wore sensible close or retriever clips but sported terrier-like whiskers.

Another interesting facet of the geneology of the Poodle is the fact that the water dogs (or spaniels) that played so large a part in the ancestral picture, and whose general type the Poodle greatly mirrors, as well as the early Newfoundland, were both broken or parti-colored breeds. Thus parti-color is a basic Poodle color. In fact, the painting of a Poodle in the classic Continental clip, owned by the Spanish royal family and done by the Spanish artist, Francisco Michens at the beginning of the 19th century, definitely depicts a parti-colored animal. Parti is a basic color factor in the breed and is the reason why it comes to the surface when least expected, and why a parti-colored Poodle, bred to a solid color, can produce solid-colored puppies. It was due only to constant and intense selection away from broken color patterns that the solid colored Poodle evolved.

In Germany, beside the Gross and Schaf Poodles formerly mentioned, there were the *Mittler* (middle or medium size), *Kleine* (little), *Kleine Pinsch* (little monkey), and *Schnur* (corded) Poodles. French classifications include the Giant, or Royal Poodle, weighing about 60 pounds, the Standard, at about 25 pounds, and the Miniature or smallest of the French Poodles. Incidently, in Germany sporting men also use a Pudelpointer for hunting upland birds which is, of course, a cross between a Poodle (Pudel) and Pointer.

The Poodle is certainly not a newcomer to the family of dog breeds. Discounting the tales of dogs which bore a striking resemblance to Poodles found on Roman coins and in Egyptian bas reliefs, we do have legitimate and undeniable depictions of Poodles as part of the compositions in paintings executed by famous masters. The great German artist, Albrecht Dürer, in the 15th and 16th centuries, used Poodles frequently in his paintings and etchings. In Holland Jan Steen painted a clipped and animated Poodle in *The Dancing Dog*. Pinturicchio, the Italian master, in the latter part of the 15th century gave colorful evidence in his paintings of the existence of the Poodle in Italy at that time. Reinagle in England, illustrator of the *Sportsman's Cabinet* in 1803, drew a picture of a "water dog" which is unmistakably a Poodle, and this was one of the first times the Poodle was mentioned in England. All this evidence, and much more,

Ch. Carillon Dilemma, owned and bred by the late Blanche Saunders. This black Standard distinguished himself with equal success in conformation and obedience competition. Photo by Evelyn Shafer.

clearly indicates that not only was the Poodle an established breed during the times mentioned, but even some of the varied clips similar to those in use today, were already used to bring style and uniqueness to the breed.

Actually it was not until 1825 that the name Poodle was substantially used to identify the breed in Britain. In Stonehenge's *Dogs of the British Islands*, an authoritative tome of its day, the Poodle was divided into two classes regardless of size; one class was composed of Poodles used as gundogs, the other classification was for pets and performing dogs. Later this classification was changed according to coat properties and divided into corded and curly varieties.

There has been a theory advanced that the Poodle initially migrated westward from Russia and that there was a cross of basic Poodle stock to a large breed of Mountain dog from the Carpathian or Pyrenees Mountains. The author instead leans toward the inclusion of the Newfoundland type mentioned earlier, which is from the same basic Mastiff stock as the Mountain dogs. The inclusion of these Mountain Dog strains in the Poodle's geneology would have detracted from the recognized aquatic ability of the Poodle instead of enhancing it, and would have introduced a blockiness and heaviness through the skull that could not have been bred out in so short a time.

Ultimately arriving in France during the wars of the First Empire, the Poodle took hold in that country and was bred pure in lineage and type for untold generations. That purity existed until modern times when, in the smaller sizes, Maltese blood was introduced to get and hold the smaller "sleeve" size of the toys, and a Bedlington Terrier cross was supposedly utilized to bring the silver-gray color

Ch. Jerlis Jump for Joy, owned by Gerald E. Siberg.
Photo by Evelyn Shafer.

to the Poodle coat, not as some authorities have stated, that it was incorporated to make the Poodle a better truffle hound, an occupation at which the breed excelled in Europe. The author could not find any explicit data in reference to this Bedlington Terrier cross. It is quite possible that a color mutation occurred in the black series, a dilution factor, which first brought gray to the coat of the breed. It is not only possible, it is indeed much more plausible.

On the Continent the author quizzed many breeders, veterinarians, and judges, and the concensus of opinion is that the French breeders have kept their Poodles at a generally high standard of intelligence and have held, more firmly, the true Poodle personality. They also can be given full credit for the evolution of the pure white Poodle. Incidently, there was a tiny sleeve type toy, developed in Cuba and called the White Cuban. It was introduced to Spain and imported from there to England where, in the 18th century, it became quite a popular favorite. English Poodles are more elegant and refined than those on the Continent. British breeders have also developed a

Arianne's Petite Zee Zee, owned by Muriel and Richard Hucknall. Photo by Evelyn Shafer.

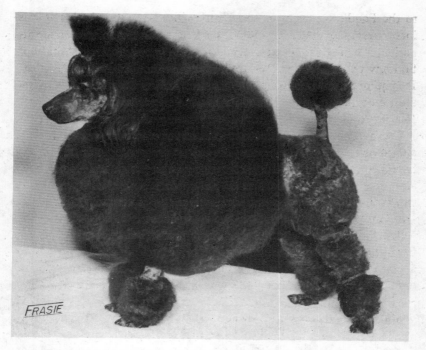

Ch. Chocolate Bud de Bur Mar, owned by Mrs. Jane Fitts.
Photo by Frasie.

more finely chiseled head in both Standards and Miniatures. The breed in America is noted throughout the rest of the world for the quality and quantity of their unsurpassed coats. We have, in America, also developed toys that are without peers anywhere else in the world.

The whole history of the breed points toward its extreme intelligence, adaptability, cleverness, and intense and quick desire for the dog to please his master. This is a dog born and bred to many tasks, and possessing an intellectual ability so great, combined with such a gay and happy physical speed in the accomplishment of any and all the tasks that it has done and, in remote places is still doing, that it has lost its heritage somewhere along the way. The Poodle essentially no longer hunts, or herds, or pulls carts, or performs any of the utilitarian services once rendered unto man. And, strangely enough, it was man who was the Poodle's undoing, who removed him from the realm of the sporting or working dog. Man took that extreme intelligence and ability to learn quickly, plus the laughing personality, the eager vitality, and turned this fine sporting and working breed into a clown, a trick dog par excellence, seen and known on vaudeville stages and under circus canvas throughout the world.

Yet, in the end result, this proved to be not a disservice at all, to either the breed or to mankind. It simply led to specialization in another and greater field for this sagacious and unconquerable breed.

There are in the world, a great mass of people who love dogs, large dogs, medium-sized ones, and small dogs. These people do not wish to hunt, nor do they own or herd sheep, or work in circuses or on the stage. They are just ordinary, dog loving people, even as you and I. They want a dog for a pet and companion. A smart dog, a good looking dog that they can be proud of, a dog that can fit in nicely with their family and their way of life. What better breed can be found for this major purpose than the Poodle? Three sizes and many colors, and always intelligent, easy to teach, eager to learn. Beauty, cleanliness and superb intelligence makes the Poodle the ultra-ideal as a pet, companion and housedog and, in this field, in this specialty, he has no peer.

There is no other breed more fitted for bench show competition than the Poodle, either, for he is, when fully barbered and in his prime, the epitome of showy elegance—the show dog supreme. The breed's many group and best-in-show wins prove its ability in this area of canine endeavor. Of course the breed's unsurpassed intelligence and trainability make its prowess in obedience competition an accepted fact.

For all the Poodle's many accomplishments and physical appeal the breed found it rather difficult to gain a popularity foothold in America due to the decidedly erroneous public opinion that it was a pampered pet and a performing clown. The Poodle Club was formed in 1876 and struggled along through unfruitful years until 1930 when a hard core of true and ambitious fanciers helped to bring the breed to the fore in American dogdom.

Through hard work and by bringing the true story of the Poodle and his enduring and endearing abilities to a dog-conscious public, these earnest breeders brought the Poodle to the pinnacle it now justly occupies as the most popular dog breed in the United States.

Changes have been made over the years toward a greater perfection of form. Miniatures crossed with toys and the smallest of the resulting litters used for breeding have moved these tiny beauties away from the nondescript conformation brought by Maltese crosses and to a standard of small Poodle elegance not before achieved. Today Poodles in all three size categories are animals of true and lasting beauty.

The author in his travels has found Poodles everywhere, in all parts of the globe. The Poodle has become the breed of the people, of special, fastidious people who want in their pet and companion, in this important member of the family group, the utmost in beauty, intelligence and that certain something of character that only the Poodle has . . . and gives.

Chapter 2
The Riddle of Inheritance

In 1859 Charles Robert Darwin's startling book on the origin of species was published. Darwin's theory of evolution changed man's concept of himself and the world around him. Science knew then that natural selection produced changes in the inheritable patterns of all living things. But, both Darwin and other scientists asked, "How do these changes come about? What causes them?" There seemed to be no rules, nothing that could be considered definite, no design that could be followed to an end result. There had to be a pattern of inheritance. But, what was it? How did it work?

Darwin did not know that his basic laws of evolution and those of heredity were being developed at approximately the same time, and that the answers he sought would become a science in its own right, the science of genetics.

Genetics, the study of inheritance in living things, is actually the science of life itself. The ability to best make use of the various known breeding procedures is the key to all breeding success. Most laymen retreat from the word "genetics" as something which is beyond the scope of their understanding. Few, if any, dog breeders are scientists, geneticists or mathematicians, and they need not be for understanding of the fundamentals. In this chapter and the next will be found all you need to know about the fascinating subjects of genetics and breeding techniques, written so that the lay reader can understand and, what is more important, make use of the basic precepts.

Before we begin to delve into the riddle of inheritance, we must first clear away the debris of old untruths and superstition so that we may see clearly the true structure that lies beyond. The inheritance of acquired characteristics is one of the fallacious theories that was

Ch. Sudbrook Sunday Go T' Meeting, owned by Harmo Kennels and bred by Mrs. S. Cox. Sire: Sudbrook Sunday Special; dam: Sudbrook Tophill Sundancer. Photo by Evelyn Shafer.

Ch. St. Aubrey Tiderace Shoeshine Boy, owned by Harmo Kennels and bred by Mrs. J. E. P. Brass. Sire: Tophill Toyboy; dam: Tiderace Sparklet of Fircot. Photo by Evelyn Shafer.

widely believed and has its disciples even today. Birthmarking is another false theory which must be discarded in the light of present-day genetical knowledge. The genes which give our dogs all their inheritable material are protected from almost every environmental influence. What the host does or has done to him in the normal course of his life influences them not at all.

Telegony is another of the untrue beliefs about influencing inherited characteristics. This is the theory that the sire of one litter could or would influence the progeny of a future litter out of the same bitch but sired by an entirely different stud. Telegony is, in its essence, comparable to the theory of saturation—which is the belief that if a bitch is bred many times in succession to the same stud, she will become so "saturated" with his "blood" that she will produce only puppies of his type, even when mated to an entirely different stud. By far the strongest and most widely believed superstition was

Ch. Edri's Bet A Million, owned by Mrs. Priscilla Richardson. This black Miniature is shown winning first in the Non-Sporting group at the Elm City Kennel Club under judge William Ackland; handler Wendell Sammet. Photo by Evelyn Shafer.

Ch. Chenue de la Fontaine, owned by Dr. and Mrs. A. Stehr. This white Standard won first in the Non-Sporting group at the Kennel Club of Northern New Jersey under judge William Ackland, handler William Trainor. Photo by Evelyn Shafer.

the theory that the blood was the vehicle through which all inheritable material was passed from parents to offspring, from one generation to the next. The taint of that supersition still persists in such breeding terms as "bloodlines," "percentage of blood," "pure-blooded," "blue-blooded," etc. This "blood" reference in regard to heredity crops up in all places and for all allied references, as witness the politician who cries vehemently, "I am proud that the blood of Paul Revere runs in my veins!" To achieve such a remarkable accomplishment would require transfusion from a long-dead corpse.

The truth was found in spite of such a persistent theory, and in the history of science there is no more dramatic story than that of the discovery of the true method of inheritance. No, the truth was not arrived at in some fine endowed scientific laboratory gleaming with the mysterious implements of research. The scene was instead a small dirt garden in Moravia, which is now a part of Czechoslovakia. Here Gregor Johann Mendel, a Moravian monk, planted and crossed several varieties of common garden peas and quietly recorded the differences that occurred through several generations. Over a period of eight years this remarkable man continued his studies. Then, in 1865, he read a paper he had prepared regarding his experiments to a society of historians and naturalists. The society subsequently published this paper in its journal, which was obscure and definitely limited in distribution.

Now we come to the amazing part of this story, for Mendel's theory of inheritance, which contained the fundamental laws upon which all modern advances in genetics have been based, gathered dust for 34 years, and it seemed that one of the most important scientific discoveries of the nineteenth century was to be lost to mankind. Then in 1900, 16 years after Mendel's death, the paper was rediscovered and his great work given to the world.

In his experiments with the breeding of garden peas, Mendel discovered the underlying elements of heredity. He found that when two individual plants which differed in a unit trait were mated, one trait appeared in the offspring and one did not. The trait which was

Ch. Tydel's Dancing Girl, owned by the late Marguerite Tyson. Dancing Girl was one of the top winners of the breed during her show career. She is seen winning the Toy group at the Tampa Bay Kennel Club under judge James W. Trullinger, handler Maxine Beam. Photo by Evelyn Shafer.

	SIRE AND DAM		PROGENY			

MENDELIAN EXPECTATION CHART
The six possible ways in which a pair of determiners can unite.
Ratios apply to expectancy over large numbers, except in lines no.
1, 2 and 6 where exact expectancy is realized in every litter.

visible he named the "dominant" trait, and the one which was not visible he called the "recessive" trait. He proposed that traits, such as color, are transmitted by means of units in the sex cells and that one of these units must be pure, let us say either black or white, but never be a mixture of both. From a black parent which is pure for that trait, only black units are transmitted, and from a white parent, only white units can be passed down. But when one parent is black and one is white, a hybrid occurs which transmits both the black and white units in equal amounts. The hybrid itself will take the color of the dominant parent, yet carry the other color as a recessive. Various combinations of unit crosses were tried by Mendel, and he found that there were six possible ways in which a pair of determiners (Mendel's "units") could combine with a similar pair. This simple Mendelian law holds true in the actual breeding of all living things—of plants, mice, humans, or Poodles.

The beginning of new life in mammals arises from the union of a male sperm and a female egg cell during the process of breeding.

Each sperm cell has a nucleus containing one set of chromosomes, which are small packages, or units, of inheritable material. Each egg also possesses a nucleus and a set of chromosomes. The new life formed by the union of sperm cell and egg cell then possesses two sets of chromosomes—one from the sperm, one from the egg, or one set from the sire and one set from the dam. For when the sperm cell enters the egg, it does two things—it starts the egg developing and it adds a set of chromosomes to the set already in the egg. Here is the secret of heredity, for on the chromosomes lie the genes, the units that shape the destiny of the unborn young. Thus we see that the pattern of heredity, physical and mental, is transmitted to our dog from its sire and dam through tiny complex units called genes, which are the connecting links between the puppy and his ancestors.

These packets of genes, the chromosomes, resemble long, paired strings of beads. Each pair is alike, the partners formed the same, yet differing from the like partners of the next pair. In the male we find the exception to this rule, for here there is one pair of chromo-

Ch. Crikora Calamity Jane, owned by Wilbramont Kennels. A black Miniature, this bitch was best of variety at the Westchester Kennel Club, scoring from the classes. She made this impressive win under judge Edward Jenner, handler Jane F. Kamp. Photo by Evelyn Shafer.

Ch. J. C. Fabulous Fanny, owned by Mrs. A. C. Pearson. This black Toy bitch boasts a proud record of top wins. She is shown scoring best of variety at the Poodle Club of Massachusetts under English judge Mrs. E. Conn, handler Anne Rogers Clark. Photo by Evelyn Shafer.

somes composed of two that are not alike. These are the sex chromosomes, and in the male they are different from those in the female in that the female possesses a like pair while the male does not. If we designate the female chromosomes as X, then the female pair is XX. The male too has an X chromosome, but its partner is a Y chromosome. If the male X chromosome unites with the female X chromosome, then the resulting embryo will be a female. But if the male Y chromosome is carried by the particular sperm that fertilizes the female egg, the resulting progeny will be a male. It is, therefore, a matter of chance as to what sex the offspring will be, since the sperm is capricious and fertilization is random. Although other cells in the body of the parent dogs contain the chromosomes in pairs, the sperm and eggs contain single chromosomes, and consequently single genes.

The actual embryonic growth of the puppy is a process of division of cells to form more and more new cells; at each cell division of the fertilized egg each of the two sets of chromosomes provided by sire and dam also divide, until all the myriad divisions of cells and chromosomes have reached an amount necessary to form a complete and living entity. Then birth becomes an accomplished fact, and we see before us a living, squealing Poodle puppy.

What is he like, this puppy? He is what his controlling genes have made him. His sire and dam have contributed one gene of each kind to their puppy, and this gene which they have given him is but one of the two which each parent possesses for a particular characteristic. Since he has drawn these determiners at random, they can be either dominant or recessive genes. His dominant heritage we can see when he develops, but what he possesses in recessive traits is hidden.

There are rules governing dominant and recessive traits useful in summarizing what is known of the subject at the present time. We can be reasonably sure that a dominant trait: (1) Does not skip a generation. (2) Will affect a relatively large number of the progeny. (3) Will be carried only by the affected individuals. (4) Will minimize the danger of continuing undesirable characteristics in a strain. (5) Will make the breeding formula of each individual quite certain.

With recessive traits we note that: (1) The trait may skip one or more generations. (2) On the average a relatively small percentage of the individuals in the strain carry the trait. (3) Only those individuals which carry a pair of determiners for the trait exhibit it. (4) Individuals carrying only one determiner can be ascertained only by mating. (5) The trait must come through both sire and dam.

You will hear some breeders say that the bitch contributes 60 percent or more to the excellence of the puppies. Others swear that the influence of the sire is greater than that of the dam. Actually, the puppy receives 50 percent of his germ plasm from each, though one parent may be so dominant that it seems that the puppy received most of his inheritable material from that parent. From the fact that the puppy's parents also both received but one set of determiners from each of their parents and in turn have passed on but one of their sets to the puppy, it would seem that one of those sets that the grandparents contributed has been lost and that therefore the puppy has inherited the germ plasm from only two of its grandparents, not four. But chromosomes cross over, and it is possible for the puppy's four grandparents to contribute an equal 25 percent of all the genes

Chromosomes in nucleus of cell.

Chromosomes arranged in pairs, showing partnership.

inherited, or various and individual percentages, one grandparent contributing more and another less. It is even possible for the pup to inherit no genes at all from one grandparent and 50 percent from another.

The genes that have fashioned this puppy of ours are of chemical composition and are vital units securely isolated from most outside influences, a point which we have made before and which bears repeating. Only certain kinds of man-directed radiation, some poisons, or other unnatural means can cause change in the genes. Environment can effect an individual but not his germ plasm. For instance, if the puppy's nutritional needs are not fully provided for during his period of growth, his end potential will not be attained, but regardless of his outward appearance, his germ plasm remains inviolate and capable of passing on to the next generation the potential that was denied him by improper feeding.

Breeding fine Poodles would be a simple procedure if all characteristics were governed by simple Mendelian factors, but alas, this is not so. Single genes are not always responsible for single characteristics, mental or physical. The complexity of any part of the body and its dependence upon other parts in order to function properly makes it obvious that we must deal with interlocking blocks of controlling genes in a life pattern of chain reaction. Eye color, for instance, is determined by a simple genetic factor, but the ability to see, the complicated mechanism of the eye, the nerves, the blood supply, the retina and iris, even how your Poodle reacts to what he sees, are all part of the genetic pattern of which eye color is but a segment.

Ch. Legagwann Altair of Old Ivy, owned by George J. Wanner.
Photo by Evelyn Shafer.

Since they are chemical in makeup themselves, the genes can and do change. In fact, it is thought now that many more gene changes take place than were formerly suspected, but that the great majority are either within the animal, where they cannot be seen, or are so small in general scope that they are overlooked. The dramatic changes which affect the surface are the ones we notice and select for or against according to whether they direct us toward our goal or away from it. Again, with the vagary inherent in all living things, the altered gene can change once again back to its original form. The loss of a gene or the gain of a gene, or the process of change among the genes, is known as mutation, and the animal affected is called a mutant.

We see then that the Poodle puppy is the product of his germ plasm, which has been handed down from generation to generation. We know that there are certain rules that generally govern the pattern that the genes form and that a gene which prevents another gene from showing in an individual is said to be a dominant and the repressed gene a recessive. Remember, the animal itself is not dominant or recessive in color or any other characteristic. It is the gene that is dominant or recessive, as judged by results. We find that an animal can contain in each of his body cells a dominant and a recessive gene. When this occurs, the dog is said to be heterozygous. We know that there is an opposite to the heterozygous individual, an animal which contains two genes of the same kind in its cells—either two dominants or two recessives—and this animal is said to be homozygous.

Every bitch that stands before us, every stud we intend to use, is not just one dog, but two. Every living thing is a Jekyll and Hyde, shadow and substance. The substance is the dog that lives and breathes and moves before us, the animal that we see, the physical manifestation of the interaction of genotypic characters and environment—the "phenotype." The shadow is the Poodle we don't see, yet this shadow is as much a part of the dog before us as the animal we see. This shadow-dog is the gene-complex, or total collection of its genes—the "genotype." The visual substance is easily evaluated, but the invisible shadow must also be clearly seen and evaluated,

Ch. Harmo Divot, owned by Harmo Kennels. Photo by Evelyn Shafer.

for both shadow and substance contribute equally to the generations to come. Without understanding the complete genetic picture of any particular dog, we cannot hope to successfully use that dog to accomplish specific results. In order to understand, we must delve into the genetic background of the animal's ancestry until the shadow becomes as clearly discernible as the substance and we can evaluate the dog's genetic worth as a whole, for this dog that stands before us is but the containing vessel, the custodian of a specific pattern of heredity.

I have tried to present to you a working knowledge of the process of inheritance, picking the most pertinent aspects from the great amount of literature pertaining to this subject. If you wish to delve deeper into this most fascinating of all sciences, you will find in the bibliography books of much greater scope than we could cram into this one chapter. But before we leave the subject, a few more important phases must be examined. One is the relationship of animal to man in regard to genetics. Though man is an animal and follows the pattern of genetic inheritance precisely as the lower animals do, we must not fashion a parallel between the two. Animals have only biological heredity, while man is greatly influenced by a very complicated and demanding cultural or social inheritance. In our breeding operations of domestic animals we can select, but the mesh of civilization which man has woven around himself does not allow for natural selection except in extreme cases. Though social inheritance is not transmitted through the chromosomes, being an acquired characteristic, it is nevertheless linked with inheritance in that it is absorbed by the reasoning human brain. Here is the great difference between man and animal. Man can reason and invent, the animal cannot. Man conquers environment through imagination, reasoning, and invention; the animal either dies or adapts itself through changes in function and bodily structure.

Breeds have inborn genetic aptitudes which become manifest only when exposed to specific environmental influences. Poodles, given a chance, will exhibit certain inherited characteristics that will interest, and in some cases amaze, breeders and owners. Easy adaptation to water work has been previously mentioned. The breed also has a definite fondness for retrieving. This combination of aptitudes, associated with the Poodle's protective coat, can result in a very fine duck-hunting water dog.

Ch. Lady Margaret of Belle Glen, owned by Mrs. James Cosden and handled by Richard Bauer. A best in show winner, Lady Margaret is presented in the ring in the Continental clip. Photo by Evelyn Shafer.

Poodles will often tree game with all the verve and sureness of hounds bred particularly for this purpose. Because of this inherited aptitude, Poodles quite frequently make excellent squirrel dogs. Indeed, it would not be too difficult to transport a good, rugged Standard Poodle, who possesses this natural aptitude, from the show ring to the woods for a bit of fine fall sport with his owner. Believe me, this concept is not too farfetched.

Selection for such aptitudes, or for other known genetic traits, will serve to accent them or "fix" them in your strain. Watch for indications of these traits, or for change within a specific line. Change is constant and is a part of progress and of life, but it must be upward toward greater merit and perfection or it brings us to retrogression. The pattern of heredity must be clearly seen and understood if progress is to be made in breeding activity, and that pattern cannot be known unless it is unveiled and the faults as well as the virtues, dominant and recessive, are revealed and honestly evaluated.

These Poodles are typical of the type bred in France and other parts of Continental Europe. United Press Int'l.

With the basic concept of heredity that Mendel discovered as a foundation, other scientists went forward to fantastic new discoveries. Genetics became a science in its own right and the men of intellect who studied, experimented and dedicated their lives to this young science were called geneticists.

The units of inheritance, the genes, were studied and their behavior catalogued. Mutations were recognized and understood. But the makeup, the chemistry of the gene itself remained a mystery. But not for long. It was discovered that there was a chemical powder called deoxyribonucleic acid, named DNA for handiness, and another nucleic acid called RNA (ribonucleic acid) in chromosomes that were, with protein, the materials of heredity. DNA is a genetic Svengali, with complete domination over all living cells and able to constantly reproduce itself, a process startlingly unique. RNA is much like it in scope. So tiny that it requires an enormous electronic microscope to become visible. RNA is yet so omniscient that it contains within itself the creative diversity to command uncountable billions of forms through its composition. The power, almost unbelievable in scope, that it commands is due to the 4 nucleotides of which it is composed. These nucleotides, in turn, produce 20 universal amino acids, which themselves produce over 100,000 proteins which give shape, form and substance to the infinite diversity of life-forms we know of on earth.

The study of genetics still goes on as men of science delve deeper and deeper into cause and effect. What we know today of inheritance is of immeasurable importance in animal breeding, removing a great deal of the guesswork from our operations. Yet we do not know enough to make the breeding of top stock a cut-and-dried matter, or to reduce it to the realm of pure science, with a definite answer to every problem. Perhaps this is where the fascination lies. Life is spontaneous and many times unstable, so that even with the greater knowledge that the future will no doubt bring, it is possible that the breeding of top animals will still remain a combination of science and art, with a touch of necessary genius and aesthetic innovation, to ever lend fascination to this riddle of inheritance.

Chapter 3
Basic Breeding Techniques

In this modern world of rapid pace, specialization and easy, varied entertainment, artistic activity and creativeness have been lost to the ordinary individual. Self expression is a natural need of man, and we who breed dogs are extremely fortunate, for in the process we can give full rein to that inherent and necessary creativeness, to express our needs, our personalities, in living flesh and beauty. We have the power to create an animate work of art if we skillfully use the proven tools that are ready to our hands. These tools are the knowledge of genetics discussed in the last chapter and the basic breeding techniques that have been used with success in all forms of livestock breeding.

Now that we have absorbed some of the basic facts of heredity, we can, with greater understanding, examine the various kinds of breeding which can be used in perpetuating wanted characteristics. We have learned that within the design of the germ plasm great variation occurs. But within the breed itself as a whole, we have an average, or norm, which the great majority of Poodles mirror. Draw a straight horizontal line on a piece of paper and label this line "norm." Above this line draw another and label it "above norm." This latter line represents the top dogs, the great ones, and the length of this line will be very much shorter than the length of the "norm" line. Below the "norm" line draw still another line, designating this to be "below norm." These are the animals possessing faults which we do not wish to perpetuate.

Since the time of the first registered Poodle the number of breeders who have molded the characteristics of the breed both here and abroad have been legion. So many have bred without a basic knowledge of any of the fundamentals that the stock produced has the detrimental effect of dangerously lowering the norm. Examine the

Ch. Puttencove Playboy, owned by Puttencove Kennels and bred by the owner and Kathleen Baker. Sire: Ch. Chantilly Lover Boy; dam: Ch. Puttencove Diantha. Photo by Evelyn Shafer.

pedigrees of your dogs, and in many instances you will find an example of this—a line incorporated in your pedigree that causes worry to the true student of breeding. The real objective of all breeding is to raise the norm of a given breed and thereby approach always closer to the breed standard.

If we are to achieve the greatest good from any program of breeding, there are four important traits which we must examine. It is essential that these traits should never depart from the norm.

The first is fertility. The lack of this essential in any degree must be guarded against diligently.

The second is vigor. Loss of vigor, or hardiness, and its allied ills, such as lowered resistance to disease, finicky eating, etc., will lead to disaster.

Longevity is the third important trait. An individual of great worth —who represents a fortunate combination of excellent characteristics which he passes on to his offspring—must be useful for a long time after his worth is recognized by the progeny produced.

The fourth is temperament. Lack of true Poodle character nullifies any other advances which you may make in your breeding program.

The norm can be likened to the force of gravity, possessing a powerful pull toward itself, so that regression toward the average is strong, even though you have used breeding parents which are both above average. The same holds true for progeny bred from animals below norm, but from these you will get a lesser number which reach the mean average and a greater number which remain below norm. In case of the better-than-average parents, some of the progeny

Ch. Wayne Valley Sir Galahad, owned by Wayne Valley Kennels. This white Toy is seen in a win of Toy group first at the Clearwater Kennel Club under judge E. D. McQuown, handler Anne Rogers Clark. Photo by Evelyn Shafer.

Ch. Highland Sand George, owned by James Farrel. This black Miniature was best of breed at the specialty show of the Cavalier Poodle Club under judge Reginald Sparkes, handler Tom Crowe. Photo by Evelyn Shafer.

will stay above the norm line and the majority will regress. Occasionally a dog of superior structure is produced by a poor family, but inevitably this animal is useless as a stud because he will produce all his objectionable family traits and none of the fortuitous characteristics he displays in himself. From a breeding standpoint it is far better to use an average individual from top stock than a top individual from average or below-average stock. It is also true that many times a great show dog produces average progeny while his little-known brother, obscured by the shadow of the great dog's eminence, produces many above-average young. This is not as strange as it sounds when we consider the fact that the individual animal is the custodian of his germ plasm and it is this germ plasm that produces, not the individual. In this instance, due to variation in the germ plasm, the top dog does not possess the happy genetic combinations that his average brother does and so cannot produce stock of comparative value.

Ch. Fieldstreams Bojangles, owned by Audrey Watts Kelch. This black Toy was best in show at the Longshore-Southport Kennel Club under judge Len Carey, handler Ben Burwell. Photo by Evelyn Shafer.

Any of the various categories of breeding practice which we will outline can be followed for the betterment of the breed if used intelligently. Regardless of which practice one follows, there generally comes a time when it is necessary to incorporate one or more of the other forms into the breeding program in order to concentrate certain genetic characters or to introduce new ones which are imperative for over-all balance. Outcross breeding is not recommended as a consistent practice. Rather, it is a valuable adjunct to the other methods when used as a corrective measure. Yet outcross breeding in the Poodle does not, as would be supposed from definition, produce completely heterozygous young. The root stock of the breed is the same regardless of which breeding partners are used and, as we have previously shown, much of the stock which represents what we term outcross breeding shows some common ancestry within a few generations.

INBREEDING

By breeding father to daughter, half brother to half sister, son to mother, and, by closest inbreeding of all, brother to sister, stability and purity of inherited material is obtained. Specifically, inbreeding concentrates both good features and faults, strengthening dominants and bringing recessives out into the open where they can be seen and evaluated. It supplies the breeder with the only control he can have over prepotency and homozygosity, or the combining and balancing of similar genetic factors. Inbreeding does not produce degeneration, it merely concentrates weaknesses already present so that they can be recognized and eliminated. This applies to both physical and psychical hereditary transmission.

The most important phases of inbreeding are: (1) To choose as nearly faultless partners as is possible; (2) To cull, or select, rigidly from the resultant progeny.

Selection is always important regardless of which breeding procedure is used, but in inbreeding it becomes imperative. It is of

Ch. Kenbrook Forest Vodka, owned by Dr. Ralph A. Logan and Edward B. Jenner. A blue Toy, this dog is shown in a win of best in show at the Catonsville Kennel Club under judge William L. Kendrick, handler Richard Bauer. Photo by Evelyn Shafer.

interest to note that the most successful inbreeding programs have used as a base an animal which was either inbred or line-bred. To the breeder, the inbred animal represents an individual whose breeding formula has been so simplified that certain results can almost always be depended upon.

There are many examples of extreme inbreeding over a period of generations in other animal and plant life. Perhaps the most widely known are the experimental rats bred by Dr. Helen L. King, which are the result of over one hundred generations of direct brother and sister mating. The end result has been bigger, finer rodents than the original pair, and entirely dependable uniformity. Dr. Leon F. Whitney has bred and developed a beautiful strain of tropical fish, *Lebistes reticulatus*, commonly known as "guppies," by consecutive brother to sister breeding for ten generations. Dr. Whitney found that each succeeding generation was a little smaller and less vigorous, but that in the fifth generation a change occurred for the better, and in each generation thereafter size, vigor and color improved.

Ch. Cartlane Once, owned by Miriam Hall. Tauskey Photo.

This pattern should hold true with all life forms developed from the same type of breeding.

It is interesting to note that genetic experiments with plants, fish and other animals which we consider lower in the evolutionary scale than our beloved dogs have shown that when two intensely inbred lines of consecutive brother and sister matings are crossed, the resultant progeny are larger than the original heterozygous stock and possess hybrid vigor (heterosis) such as the mongrel possesses, which enables him to exist even under environmental neglect.

Can Poodle breeders indulge in such concentrated inbreeding with our stock, as has been attempted successfully by scientists with other genetic material? We don't know, simply because, to our knowledge, it has never been tried. It would be an expensive undertaking to keep two or more lines progressing of direct brother and sister inbreedings, to cull and destroy, always keeping the best pair as breeding partners for the next generation. Lethal faults, hitherto unsuspected in the stock, might become so drastically concentrated as to bring the experiment to a premature conclusion, even if one had the time, money and energy to attempt it. But such is the inherent character of germ plasm that one direct outcross can bring complete normality to an inbred line drastically weakened by its own concentrated faults.

It is essential that the breeder have a complete understanding of the merits of inbreeding, for by employing it skillfully results can be obtained to equal those found in other animal-breeding fields. We must remember that inbreeding in itself creates neither faults nor virtues; it merely strengthens and fixes them in the resulting animals. If the basic stock used is generally good, possessing but few faults, and those minor, then inbreeding will concentrate all those virtues which are so valuable in that basic stock. Inbreeding gives us great breeding worth by its unique ability to produce prepotency and unusual similarity of type. It exposes the "skeletons in the closet" by bringing to light hitherto hidden faults, so that they may be selected against. We do not correct faults by inbreeding, therefore, we merely make them recognizable so they can be eliminated. The end result of inbreeding, coupled with rigid selection, is complete stability of the breeding material.

With certain strains inbreeding can be capricious, revealing organic weaknesses never suspected that result in decreased vitality, abnormalities—physical and mental—or lethal or crippling factors. Unfortunately, it is not possible to foretell results when embarking on such a program, even if seemingly robust and healthy breeding partners are used as a base. The best chance of success generally comes from the employment of animals which themselves have been strongly inbred and have not been appreciably weakened by it in any way.

An interesting development frequently found in inbreeding is in the extremes produced. The average progeny from inbreeding is equal to the average from line-breeding or outbreeding, but the extremes are greater than those produced by either of the latter breeding methods. Inbreeding, then, is at once capable of producing the best and the worst, and these degrees can be found present in the same litter.

Here again, in inbreeding, as in most of the elements of animal

Denbur's Another New Hat, owned by Mrs. G. M. Caskey, Jr.
Photo by Evelyn Shafer.

Ch. Hollycourt Talent of Silver, owned by Miss M. Ruelle Kelchner. Photo by Evelyn Shafer.

husbandry, we must avoid thinking in terms of human equations. Whether for good or ill, your Poodle was man-made, and his destiny and that of his progeny lie in your hands. By selection you improve the strain, culling and killing misfits and monsters. Mankind indulges in no such practice of purification of the race. He mates without any great mental calculation or plan for the future generation. His choice of a mate is both geographically and socially limited in scope. No one plans this mating of his for the future betterment of the breed. Instead, he is blindly led by an emotion labeled "love," and sometimes by a lesser romantic, "desire." For our Poodles we want something vastly better than the hit-and-miss proposition that has been the procedure of man.

Another type of inbreeding, which is not practiced as much as it should be, is "backcrossing." Here we think largely in terms of the male dog, since the element of time is involved. The process involves finding a superior breeding male who is so magnificent in type that we want to perpetuate his qualities and produce, as closely as we can, the prototype of this certain individual. This good male is bred to a fine bitch, and the best female pup who is similar to her sire in type is bred back again to her sire. Again, the best female pup is selected and bred back to her sire. This is continued as long as the male can reproduce, or until weaknesses become apparent (if they do) that make it impractical to continue. If this excellent male seems to have acquired his superiority through the genetic influence of his mother, the first breeding made should possibly be the mating of son to mother, and the subsequent breedings as described above. In each litter the bitch retained to backcross to her sire should, of course, greatly mirror the sire's type.

Ch. Nibroc Vivian, owned by Mrs. C. K. Corbin.
Photo by Evelyn Shafer.

Ch. Puttencove Gay Valentino, owned by Puttencove Kennels.
Photo by Evelyn Shafer.

LINE-BREEDING

Line-breeding is a broader kind of inbreeding that conserves valuable characteristics by concentration and in a general sense gives us some control of type but a lesser control over specific characteristics. It creates "strains," or "families," within the breed which are easily recognized by their similar conformation. This is the breeding method used by most of the larger kennels, with varied success, since it is not extreme and therefore relatively safe. It is also the method the neophyte is generally advised to employ, for the same reasons.

Specifically, line-breeding entails the selection of breeding partners who have one or more common ancestors in their pedigrees. These individuals (or individual) occur repeatedly within the first four or five generations, so that it can be assumed their genetic influence molds the type of succeeding generations. It is a fact that in many breeds success has been obtained by line-breeding to outstanding individuals.

The method varies greatly in intensity, so that some dogs may be strongly line-bred, while others only remotely so. Selection is an important factor here too, for if we line-breed to procure the specific type of a certain fine animal, then we must select in succeeding generations breeding stock which is the prototype of that individual, or our reason for line-breeding is lost.

Ch. Merrymorn Lita, owned by Mrs. Milton Erlanger. Lita, a black Toy is shown winning first in the Toy group at the Mid-Hudson Kennel Club under judge Alva Rosenberg, handler Anne Rogers Clark. Photo by Evelyn Shafer.

Ch. Prankster Darius, owned by Mrs. George Marmer. He is shown winning best in show at the Middlesex County Kennel Club under judge H. P. Saunders, handler William Trainor. Photo by Evelyn Shafer.

One of the chief dangers of line-breeding can be contributed by the breeder of the strain. Many times the breeder reaches a point where he selects his breeding partners on pedigree alone, instead of by individual selection and pedigree combined within the line.

In some instances intense line-breeding, particularly when the individual line-bred to is known to be prepotent, can have all the strength of direct inbreeding.

To found a strain which has definite characteristics, within the breed, the following recommendations can be used as a guide.

1. Decide what few traits are essential and what faults are intolerable. Vigor, fertility, character, and temperament must be included in these essentials.

2. Develop a scoring system and score selected virtues and faults in accordance with your breeding aim. Particular stress should be put upon scoring for individual traits which need improvement.

3. Line-breed consistently to the best individuals produced which by the progeny test show that they will further improve the strain.

Inbreeding can be indulged in if the animal used is of exceptional quality and with no outstanding faults. Outcrossings can be made to bring in wanted characteristics if they are missing from the basic stock. Relationship need not be close in the foundation animals, since wide outcrosses will give greater variation and therefore offer a much wider selection of desirable trait combinations.

Every dog used in this breeding program to establish a strain must be rigidly assessed for individual and breeding excellence and the average excellence of its relatives and progeny.

OUTCROSS BREEDING

Outcross breeding is the choosing of breeding partners whose pedigrees, in the first five or six generations, are free from any

Ch. Braebeck Toni of Montefleuri, owned by the late Marguerite Tyson. This black Miniature import was best in show at the National Capitol Kennel Club under Mrs. Sherman R. Hoyt (left), handler Howard Tyler. Photo by Reding.

Palmarese Victoreuse, owned by Janet V. Blannin and Virginia Fugitt. This bitch is shown scoring best of winners at the Maria Obispo Kennel Club under judge Virginia Keckler, handler Mr. Fugitt. Photo by Joan Ludwig.

common ancestry. To outcross completely, using the term literally (complete heterozygosity), it would be necessary to use an individual of an alien breed as one of the breeding partners.

For the breeder to exercise any control over the progeny of an outcross mating, one of the partners should be inbred or closely line-bred. The other partner should show, in himself and by the progeny test when bred to other bitches, that he is dominant in the needed compensations which are the reasons for the outcross. Thus, by outcross breeding, we bring new and needed characteristics into a strain, along with greater vigor and, generally, a lack of uniformity in the young. Greater uniformity can be achieved if the outcross is made between animals of similar family type. Here again we have a breeding method which has produced excellent individuals, since it tends to conceal recessive genes and promote individual merit. But it generally leads to a lower breeding worth in the outbred animal by dispersing favorable genetic combinations which have given us strain uniformity.

Outcross breeding can be likened to a jigsaw puzzle. We have a puzzle made up of pieces of various shapes and sizes which, when fitted together, form a certain pattern. This basic puzzle is comparable to our line-bred or inbred strain. But in this puzzle there are a few pieces that we would like to change, and in so doing change the finished puzzle pattern for the better. We outcross by removing some of the pieces and reshaping them to our fancy, remembering that these new shapes also affect the shapes of the adjoining pieces, which must then be slightly altered for perfect fit. When this has been successfully accomplished, the finished pattern has been altered to suit our pleasure—we hope.

It sometimes happens that a line-bred or inbred bitch will be outcross bred to a stud possessed of an open pedigree. It would be assumed by the breeder that the bitch's family type would dominate in the resulting progeny. But occasionally the stud proves himself to be strongly prepotent, and the young instead reflect his individual qualities, not those of the bitch. This can be good or bad, depending on what you are looking for in the resultant litter.

Incidentally, when we speak of corrective, or compensation, breeding, we do not mean the breeding of extremes to achieve an intermediate effect. We would not breed an extremely shy bitch to an over aggressive or vicious stud in the hope of getting progeny of

Rogers' Arsenic and Old Lace, owned by Betty Rogers. This black Miniature is shown winning best puppy in show at the Columbine State Poodle Club specialty under judge Malcolm Phelps. Photo by Bob Machinski.

good temperament. The offspring of such a mating would show temperament faults of both the extremes. Corrective, or compensation, breeding means the breeding of one partner which is lacking, or faulty, in any specific respect, to an animal which is normal or excellent in the particular area where the other partner is found lacking. In the resulting progeny we can expect to find some young which show the desired improvement.

To sum up briefly, we find that *inbreeding* brings us a fixity of type and simplifies the breeding formula. It strengthens desirable dominants and brings hidden and undesirable recessives to the surface where they can be recognized and possibly corrected by *outcross breeding*. When we have thus established definite improvement in type by rigid selection for wanted characteristics, we *linebreed* to create and establish a strain or family line which, in various degrees, incorporates and produces the improvements which have been attained.

In this maze of genetics, we must not forget the importance of the concrete essence that stands before us. The breeding partners

Ch. Cappoquin Bon Fiston, owned by Cappoquin Kennels.
Photo by Evelyn Shafer.

must be examined as individuals in themselves, apart from the story their pedigrees tell us. For as individuals they have been fashioned by, and are the custodians of, their germ plasm, and mirror this fact in their being. Breedings made from paper study only are akin to human marriages arranged in youth by a third party without consulting the partners—they can be consummated but have small chance of success.

The importance of a pedigree lies in the knowledge we have of the individual animals involved. A 15-generation pedigree means nothing if we know nothing about the dogs mentioned. It is more important to extend your knowledge of three or four generations than to extend the pedigree itself. Of real guidance in breeding is a card-index system. This system should indicate clearly the faults and virtues of every pedigree name for at least three generations, with available information as to dominant and recessive traits and the quality of each animal's progeny. At the moment, such a system is practically impossible to achieve. There is little enough known, genetically, about living animals, and the virtues of dogs that are gone are distorted by time and sentiment. Here is a real project and a challenge for the breeder, since true pedigree recordings, correctly developed, can represent a really valuable progeny test of ancestors. To be truly efficacious, near ancestors, as well as litter mates, must also be examined for endowed traits, including color, and percentages in regard to these traits correlated and recorded in the pedigree index. From these indexes, graphs could be plotted which would indicate trends within the breed as a whole. To accomplish this design completely, a geneticist would have to be employed and furnished with absolutely truthful information.

The breeding of fine dogs is not a toy to be played with by children. For some of us it forms a nucleus of living, in the esthetic sense. We who give much of our time, thought, and energy to the production of superior stock are often disgusted and disillusioned by the breeding results of others who merely play at breeding. So often individuals long in the game advise the novice never to inbreed, but only to line-breed, since in this way the least harm can be done. There has been too much harm done already by novice breeders who should not have been encouraged to breed at all, except under the direct supervision or advice of an experienced or knowledgeable dog man.

The people who compose what we term the Poodle "fancy," belong to one of three categories: the novice, the amateur and the professional. The novice is one who has recently become enamored of the breed, a tyro, a beginner. Many of them remain in that category indefinitely, due to lack of sincerity or reluctance to learn. Others, eager to absorb all they can, soon rise above the original status.

The professional is one who makes his livelihood from the dog game. His living or employment depends in whole or part upon his kennel activities. A professional must know his business well in order to make it a success, and the earnest professional generally does, though he may occasionally be guilty of breeding for the market.

Numerically, the largest category is that of the amateur. To these individuals the breeding, showing or training of Poodles is a serious hobby. Here are the students of the breed, the people who, in most instances, are well informed, yet avid for new knowledge that will aid in breed betterment.

Highland Sand Magic Toy, owned by Highland Sand Kennels. He is shown going winners dog at the Poodle Club of America under judge Rosalind Layte, handler Jane F. Kamp. Photo by Evelyn Shafer.

Ch. Frosty Boy of Carribrook, owned by Lenton W. Sweigart. This white Toy is shown winning the Toy group at the Holyoke Kennel Club under Mrs. Sherman Hoyt, handler Anne Rogers Clark. Photo by Evelyn Shafer.

Our novice is many times a charming person who loves his dogs passionately, provides them with more fancy vitamins and supplements than honest food, and treats them with a sloppy sentimentality that even a human baby would resent. He simply can't wait to breed his lovely bitch and have those adorable puppies. Of course he hasn't the time to acquire a bit of knowledge about the breed, or about the animals in his bitch's pedigree or the stud to which he is going to breed. How then will he have the time or knowledge to care for the pregnant bitch and the subsequent litter properly? Yet inevitably he does find time to listen to the pseudo-professional advice of several self-confessed authorities. In due time this novice is possessed of from two to seven of the cutest puppies you ever saw, which will in turn be sold to other novices (Heaven help them) as show and breeding prospects.

By far the greatest menace to the future of the breed is a particular type of wealthy novice. Possessed of the wherewithal to keep and breed any number of dogs, and kennelmen to take care of them,

Ch. Hermscrest Jamal, owned, bred, and handled by Mrs. Frances Herms. This silver Miniature is shown scoring best of opposite sex at the Southern Adirondack Kennel Club under judge Marjorie Siebern. Photo by William Gilbert.

this novice blunders arrogantly forward by virtue of the authority vested in him by his bank-books and, unhampered by knowledge, breeds indiscriminately, producing litter upon litter of worthless stock. By the law of averages an occasional animal is produced that is good. By cramming show classes with other of his mediocre stock and shipping, with professional handlers, to parts of the country where major wins can be made with fewer entries, he soon has champions which are extensively advertised at stud for other novices to breed to. In the end this novice generally surprisingly and suddenly blossoms out as a full blown "authority" and judge.

What has been written above is not to be construed as a sweeping condemnation of all novices. Without a constant influx of neophyte breeders, the breed would not be in the high place it is today. Many so-called novices bring to their new breed interest a vast store of canine knowledge collected by an inquiring mind and contact with other breeds.

To repeat, the novice is generally advised by the old-time breeder to begin his new hobby with a line-bred bitch, as this is the cautious approach which leaves the least margin for error. But what of that novice who is essentially what we call a born "dog man"? That individual who, for lack of better definition, we say has a "feel" for dogs, who seems to possess an added sense where dogs are concerned?

If this person has an inquiring mind, normal intelligence, and has been associated with other breeds, then the picture of him as the true novice changes. The old-timer will find many times that this "novice" frequently possesses information that the old-timer did not even know existed. This is especially true if the tyro has been exposed to some scientific learning in fields relative to animal advancement. Even experience, which is the old-timer's last-ditch stand, is negligible, for this knowledgeable "novice" can disregard the vagaries of experience with foreknowledge of expectancy.

In most instances this type of novice doesn't begin to think of breeding, or even owning, a specimen of the breed until he has made a thorough study of background, faults, virtues and genetic characters. To him, imitation is not a prelude to success. Therefore the line-bred bitch, modeled by another's ego, is not for him. The outcross bitch, whose genetic composition presents a challenge and which, by diligent study and application of acquired knowledge, can become the fountainhead of a strain of his own, is the answer to his need.

Some of what you have read here in reference to the novice may have seemed to be cruel caricature. Actually, it is not caricature, but it is cruel and is meant to stress a point. We realize that to some novices our deep absorption in all the many aspects of breed betterment may seem silly or ridiculous. But the genetic repercussion of breeding stupidity can echo down through generations, making a mockery of our own intense, sometimes heartbreaking, and often humble, striving toward an ideal.

Chapter 4
Inheritance of Poodle Size

Size is an inherited genetic characteristic in all breeds of dogs including the Poodle. But, the inheritance of size in the Poodle gains more importance by virtue of the variety of sizes found and wanted in the breed to give us the three recognized Poodle varieties.

In the Poodle standard, size has been rather firmly fixed and, at the moment, does not vary enough to cause concern. There is, as yet, no element of an extreme, or giantism, so we need not worry about the anomalies produced by an excess of pituitary secretion, alone or accompanied by acromegaly, or any of the other ills that beset the basic functional qualities of the giant or extreme breeds. But, due to an intermixture of sizes to aid in upgrading and fixing type in Miniatures and Toys, variation in size does occur.

Modification in size will appear in all pure lines but, with the exception of the occasional individual, this deviation is well confined within reasonable limits. The closeness of the standards in Poodle size and the aforementioned mixture of sizes is what makes it a bit more difficult to control the dimensional elements in the Poodle.

Physiologically the ultimate size of an animal is governed by hormones, or secretions of the ductless glands, that are themselves genetically controlled. The glands which specifically control size are the pituitary (at the base of the brain), and the thyroid, situated in the throat. If the pituitary engages in excessive activity the result is giantism. If both these glands fail to function, the end result is dwarfism. When breeding for smallness, as in the Toy Poodle, it is the *kind* of dwarfism that is produced that is important, for there are two kinds of extreme smallness, and animals that are the result of these two kinds of dwarfism are labelled either cretins or proportionate dwarfs.

The cretin is the result of thyroid disfunction. This type of small-

Ch. Wycliffe Leroy, owned by Mrs. Robert Hawks and bred by Mrs. Jean M. Lyle. Sire: Ch. Wycliffe Thomas; Dam: Wycliffe Xtra Fancy. This black Standard was best of variety at the Poodle Club of Massachusetts under judge Nora Andrews, handler Jane F. Kamp. Photo by Evelyn Shafer.

ness is accompanied by high, domed skulls, weak muzzles, "pop" or large, protruding eyes, thin coats, and high, squeaky voices. Other physical anomalies that accompany extremes and result in unattractive specimens are generally also present in varied degrees. This is the kind of dwarfism not wanted in the Toy Poodle.

Proportionate dwarfs are produced by deficiencies of the pituitary hormones and are true midgets or miniatures, normally developed in all parts of the body. These are the canine dwarfs that are cultivated by breeders producing toys of many kinds. They are diminutive replicas of their larger relatives and just as robust and hardy despite their small stature.

The transmission of size in the Poodle is controlled by a complexity of genetic factors and can be also influenced in the end result by non-genetic conditions of environment, such as lack of proper food or illness during the growth period. Also size is polygenic in character and cannot, in any of the three manifestations known to the breeder of Poodles, be definitely labeled as either dominant or recessive in effect.

The only way to avoid annoying variation in any of these three sizes is by constantly selecting for the exact size you want, breeding only from Poodles of that size and so, in time, establishing a fixed size strain that will exhibit very little variation. The basic size categories should never be mixed. This practice, in Poodles, has been overdone long since.

One of the worst influences on size is the prediliction of some judges to select animals pushing the size limits in both Miniatures and Toys, and putting up very large dogs in the Standards. This kind of judging results in fanciers breeding and showing dogs as close to the limits as possible and then finding that inevitably a goodly portion of their puppies (and sometimes the best in the litters) begin to slip over the desired height. If, because of excellent type or coat, these oversize animals are bred from, more and more Miniatures and Toys that are over the standard height requirements result and soon the anguished breeder has lost all control over size. It is the author's opinion that a height limit should also be set for Standards before their size gets out of hand. It has happened before in other breeds.

I have become increasingly aware, in my travels, of a handy-sized Poodle that many people fancy as a house pet and companion. It is

Ch. Harmo Porgy, owned by Harmo Kennels and bred by Garper Kennels. Sire: Ch. Dar Bet's Barry De la Che; dam: Baldoria's Bit O' Brown. Photo by Evelyn Shafer.

above the 15 inch Miniature measurement, but not big enough if shown (and these dogs I speak of are never shown) to be considered Standards. This Poodle is a handy 17 to 18 inches tall. I have seen such animals in all parts of the globe from Casablanca and Beni Mellal in Africa, to New York City. There are several in the area in which I am at present living and I suspect that they are generally of French origin. *Medium* Poodles are approved on the Continent, but not in England or America. These Poodles are probably the same size as the original, first Poodle ancestors. If they came from England or America they would be the result of size disparity in normal size breeding since in these two countries this intermediate size would not have been bred for deliberately. For their purpose, as pets and companions, they are evidently thought of by many as being ideal in size.

It is easier to breed closer to the classic type, particularly in the Toy Poodle, by pushing the size limit. But to constantly do so will result in ever smaller numbers of dogs staying under the size limit upon maturity and will eventually produce the same results as mixed size breedings, that is; Standards that are too small to be Standards but too large to be Miniatures, Miniatures that are too large to be Miniatures but too small to be good Standards, and Toys that are too large to be Toys but too small to be ideal Miniatures.

Toy breeders must beware of the very tiny bitch even though they are attempting to breed the diminutive "sleeve" dogs for a specific market. The very small bitch is generally deficient in width and depth of ribbing and the pelvic development necessary for ease in whelping or the carrying of puppies. Such animals most often show the evidence of thyroid disfunction. These tiny bitches often deliver their litters of from 1 to 3 puppies only by Caesarian. It is better to use a bitch closer to the size limit and a very tiny stud dog of excellent type for production of these extra small Toys.

Neophyte breeders of small Poodle varieties, should not be surprised at the large size of the puppies at birth. Miniature and Toy puppies grow rapidly for a short period of time and then their growth slows down and practically stops. But the whelps of the larger, Standard parents continue in growth for a much longer period of time, while Miniatures and Toys reach full growth at a much earlier age.

Chapter 5

The Poodle Coat and Coat Color Inheritance

Before we enter the rather complicated realm of coat color inheritance let us first assess coat quality in the Poodle.

The coat of the Poodle has been the focal point of controversy for many years. A great many breeders have claimed, with absolute conviction, that the Poodle possesses a single coat with variance in the structure of each hair from the outer tip to the root or base. Other authorities have just as vehemently declared that the Poodle has a double coat, in common with other canine breeds, consisting of an undercoat, or waterproof, wooly, protective base-coat, and an outercoat, the so-called guard hairs, that is coarser, longer, and the coat most obvious to the observer.

Scientists who have studied coat structure in the Poodle agree that the breed is double-coated and, since their analysis is clinical and precise, we can assume that their findings are correct. The Poodle, like other canines, has a double coat.

It is true, however, that the nature and quality of the Poodle's coat is rather unique and lends itself to varied handling and designs in clipping. It has the quality and appearance of Persian lamb; it is fine, fluffy and light in texture and knots readily when not conscientiously looked after, much to the exasperation of the Poodle owner.

Many owners and breeders believe that the Poodle does not shed its hair as do other breeds. This, too, is a fallacy. The Poodle sheds its coat just as any other breed does. But, the shed hair is caught and trapped by the undercoat and packs down. This process is encouraged by owners and handlers of show dogs for the packed down, shed hair provides a strong base from which the sprouting, comparatively straight, fine guard hairs can gain support and stand out straight to form the familiar ruff of the show Poodle in an English Saddle or Continental clip.

Strains within the breed exhibit different coat qualities. When a certain color strain shows a definite change in coat for the better, it is an indication that mutation, or change, has occurred in the genes that are associated with color and length or density of coat, and that this variation was seen and selected for by the breeder and so became a fixed genetic virtue in this specific strain.

To completely clarify the above statement let us study a typical example. A breeder of white Poodles cannot get the same length of hair in her dogs' coats as does a neighboring breeder where only blacks are bred. In other ways the animals from both kennels are fairly equal. Mrs. White Poodle Breeder has been told by Mr. Black Poodle Breeder that genetically black hair in the Poodle grows longer than white hair and therefore the black dogs have longer coats than the white dogs and there is nothing that can be done about it. Mrs. White accepts this statement, as she should since it is a fact. Suddenly a white puppy appears in one of her litters that exhibits a coat every bit as long and full as any of her neighbor's black puppies. Naturally wanting to keep this desired trait she uses

Ch. Lady Bug of Yewtree, owned by Mrs. George Fiig. This diminutive silver Toy was best of variety at the Saw Mill River Kennel Club under Mrs. Sherman Hoyt, handler William Trainor. Photo by Evelyn Shafer.

Ch. Pixiecroft Sunbeam, owned by Mrs. Gardner Cassat. This bitch is probably the greatest winning apricot Poodle of all time. She retired from the show ring after winning first in the Non-Sporting group at the Westminster Kennel Club (pictured) under judge Haskell Schuffman, handler Anne Rogers Clark. Photo by Evelyn Shafer.

this dog upon maturity in a series of smart breedings that include inbreeding, backcrossing and linebreeding and, through a knowledge of basic genetics, soon has established a white, long-coated strain that becomes the envy of other white Poodle breeders and the hallmark of her kennels. She achieved this success by recognizing the mutation that occurred in her stock and selected for it and, through an intelligent breeding program fixed this wanted change in her strain.

There are several of these genetic coat quality factors that should be known by all Poodle breeders. The one mentioned in the preceding paragraph is a good example, for black hair in the coat of a Poodle *will* attain greater length than white hair. The color red acts the same as white in inhibiting hair length. Dominant coat qualities include thin coat, wavy hair, shorter hair and coarse hair. Recessive qualities would be the opposite. The chart that follows imparts these traits in their proper genetic category at a glance. Hair density (thin or thick coat), is arrived at by counting the number of hairs per square inch under a microscope.

Dominant Coat Characteristics	Recessive Coat Characteristics
Thin coat	Thick coat
Wavy hair	Straight hair
Shorter hair	Longer hair
Coarse hair	Fine hair

By using the Mendelian Expectation Chart in Chapter II it is easy to chart the coat quality you will get from any given mating. Thus two thin coated dogs, each carrying a known recessive for thick coats, will give you approximately 25% (Mendelian expectation ratio) thick coats, and so on.

COAT COLOR INHERITANCE

Coat color in the Poodle is not at all as clear-cut genetically as is coat quality, simply because breeding for type and size was more important than breeding for color. The result has been a fantastic mixture of colors that quite often brings surprising results in the whelping box. Recessives can be carried in the germ plasm for innumerable generations without becoming visually obvious. As a result two Poodles which, let us say, show only black breeding to the limit of a four or five generation pedigree can yet carry recessives that, when combined, produce other than black puppies in a litter. Black, being dominant, can mask recessives in the line for as many generations as you can count back.

There are four basic solid colors in Poodles; black, white, red and brown. All other colors are dilutions or modifications of these basic solids. From the standpoint of color variations the Poodle seems to be the most blessed of all breeds, exhibiting a dazzling array of color mutations, some with very subtle overtones such as the recessive apricot, puppies in this series being born apricot, black, brindle, apricot with black mask, apricot with black points, apricot with brown points, or brown, in each case, regardless of the color of the pup at birth, becoming an apricot upon reaching maturity,

In the case of the mature apricot that was brown at birth and has brown points, many breeders do not consider such a specimen a true apricot, feeling rather that it should be classified as a light brown or beige. Genetically it is a dilute brown. Incidently, brown-eyed, brown pointed Poodles are the result of double recessives and there-

Ch. Meisen Golden Gaite', owned by Hilda Meisenzahl. This apricot Miniature is shown scoring points enroute to his championship at the Glendale Kennel Club under judge Dr. Frank Porter Miller, handler Frank Sabella. Photo by Joan Ludwig.

fore breed true, never producing black pointed get.

In the maze of color statistics there is one fact that must be remembered. Regardless of the number of dilution factors and modifiers that can effect the color of the Poodle coat, turning it to all shades of blue and gray to almost white in the black series, and from dark chocolate to cream in the brown range, the full color in double genetic dose must always be considered dominant. Thus pure homozygous black must be considered dominant to brown and any dilution factor. A pure black bred to a pure brown, therefore, will produce only black puppies, but each pup will carry brown as a recessive. Black to blue will produce all blacks since blue is but a recessive, through a dilution factor, of black. Blue bred to browns will produce all blacks, if each partner is pure for the color they exhibit, because the black gene carried by the blue is dominant to the brown, while the factor for full and solid color carried by the brown dog is dominant to the dilute factor carried by the blue mate.

The chart that follows will aid in simplifying coat color inheritance.

Ch. St. Anthony's Coco, owned and bred by Mrs. Charles Anthony. Sire: Ch. Boarzell Boom De Ay; dam: St. Anthony's Kiki. Photo by Evelyn Shafer.

Black Orchid of Wembly Downs, owned by Mrs. Carruth Maguire.
Photo by Evelyn Shafer.

The code letters after each coat color is its genetic symbol. The capital letters in this code represent dominants and the lower case letters are recessives. Small letters or numbers above and to the right of the main code letters represent the presence of modifying genes.

Dominant Coat Colors
Self color—A^s
Black—B
Colored—C
Intense or full pigmentation—D
Extension of pigmentation—E
Gray factor—G

Unspotted—S

Nonsilver—S^1

Recessive Coat Colors
Black and tan—a^t
Brown—b
Albino—c
Dilution—d
Restriction of pigmentation—e
Absence of graying factor—g
Some white spots—s^2
Extreme white spotting—s^w
Silver—s^1

We can see from the chart that even though we call brown a basic color it is the result of a dilute factor acting upon black. Pure or snow white Poodles (showing some few black hairs in the coat) are the result of double recessives. Therefore, a pair of pure white Poodles when bred together will exert the influence of a double recessive for white and can produce nothing but pure white puppies. These whelps will be either snow white or ivory white, the latter color the result of apricot colored hair in the coat. Breed an ivory white (which, as was just stated, carries apricot hairs in its coat) and an apricot together and you will get a litter exhibiting various shades of apricot.

The breeder of whites should remember this important fact; there are recessive depigmenting genes, the extremely white piebald genes, that can cause white to spread over the entire body completely masking any base color and leaving only a few hairs of the base or original color, often so few that they cannot be found for identification by the naked eye. The true pigmentation of nose, eyes, lips and footpads will not be effected by these piebald masking genes. This accounts for the appearance of a pure black puppy in a litter produced by the breeding of a snow white Poodle and an ivory or cream Poodle. The genetic formula for this type of pure white would be s s , which would give us whites, with black points or should the white piebald factor effect a basic brown the result would be whites with brown points. The full genetic formula for both results would therefore be:

$$s^W s^W \text{ with BB} = \text{black points}$$
$$s^W s^W \text{ with bb } = \text{brown points}$$

To further complicate the picture where colors have been previously mixed is the fact that hidden or submerged colors can also be effected by dilution factors. Thus a white dog may carry a submerged black or apricot (see piebald) and both the unseen colors can be effected by as many recessive color genes as the ordinary black or apricot Poodle. For example, the masked black could be effected by a dilution factor turning the solid color to a silver. There is, incidently, a white with a dark blue skin that at birth appears to be brindled in color, exhibiting black-tipped hairs which gradually turn white upon maturity.

Restriction of pigmentation (e e) results in apricots and creams. A double dose of silver ($s^1 s^1$) causes a silvering of black or brown,

Ch. Ledahof Silverissimo, owned and bred by Ledahof Kennels. Sire: Ch. Perrevan Chimney Sweep; dam: Ledahof Silhouette. Photo by Evelyn Shafer.

or blue maltese (d d). The latter color, in turn produced by the dilution factor (d).

Black nosed apricots possess dominant genes for black which embryonic young exhibit but which are counteracted and submerged by apricot genes before birth. A third set of genes can also function in this color series that will tend to change the apricot to cream (chamois in England). When all three sets of genes are present and functioning the litter will consist of dark or light apricots and dark or light creams.

Never forget that black is a foundation color in apricots and creams and this unseen black can don the recessive genes of other colors and carry them indefinitely in an inactive state until paired with like genes. When this occurs the genes pair, become active and visible and produce color surprises in the nest.

Black nosed apricots (black pointed) can also produce brown pointed apricots as a result of the black dilution factor. Apricots with black points generally have a more lively, pinkish color reflected in their coats than do brown pointed apricots. The latter, when bred together, will breed true and never produce black pointed offspring. Apricots with black points also sometimes produce a type of black-and-tan (a^t) which gradually fades to pure apricot. This strange early color pattern is the result of inactive black-and-tan genes.

Inactive silver genes can also be carried by apricots. Since silver also claims black as a base color the action of apricot genes changes

Ch. Round Tables Avocat, owned by Round Table Kennels. This silver Miniature was first in the Non-Sporting group at the Jacksonville Dog Fancier's Ass'n under judge Marie Meyer, handler, Anne Rogers Clark. Photo by Evelyn Shafer.

Ch. Alekai Pokoi, owned and bred by Alekai Kennels. Sire: Ch. Alekai Nohea; dam: Ch. Ivardon Winter. Pokoi is many times a group and best in show winner. She is shown winning best in show at the Greater Miami Dog Club under judge A. Peter Knoop, handler Wendell Sammet. Photo by Evelyn Shafer.

the black pigment in silver to apricot or cream and the puppy, when born, shows no evidence of the hidden, recessive silver gene it carries. If or when, two such animals (apricots), each carrying the recessive silver gene, are bred together, some silvers will result.

The genes that produce apricot, it can now be seen, are the most influential that the Poodle can possess. Even the dominant black, which masks all other recessives, preventing them from functioning, does not have the genetic power that is possessed by apricot. In its presence black, brown, silver, black-and-tan, and white are all transformed into beautiful shades of varied apricot or into delicate creams.

In the United States and England practically all solid colors are approved so that we have a great variety of dilute solids such as, cinnamon, platinum, chinchilla, blue, etc. On the Continent only the basic black, brown and pure white are recognized as being colors fit for show competition. Breeding in Europe is also limited to pure color-to-color breeding. The author does not remember seeing other than solid Poodles on the Continent. In England I did see a pair of fine parti-colored Standards.

In Chapter 1 the author mentioned that the background color of the Poodle, through its ancient ancestry, was parti-colored. This primitive heritage still haunts breeders seeking purity in solid colors. Parti-colored dogs are Poodles that display more than one color in their coats, generally in an asymetrical or broken pattern. Another type, the so-called *phantom*, is solid but with a counter-color pattern such as the black-and-tan, but can appear in colors other than black-and-tan (silver and white or cream). The name phantom was coined by Count Alexis Pulaski who has long carried the banner for these outcasts of the Poodle family. Being recessives these combined colors crop up awkwardly in solid-color-bred litters. Incidentally, though they are Poodle outcasts and cannot be shown, parti-colors are accepted for registration by the A.K.C.

The difficulties of breeding for specific color have, by the time you have read this, become evident. Eternally blessed is the Poodle breeder who has a breeding line of pure color lineage. One solution offered by concerned breeders is the development of pedigrees that will name the colors of all the dogs for as many generations as the form can hold. It is a step in the right direction but the fallacy lies in the fact that recessives can be carried unseen for many more generations than the pedigree shows, and that there may have been colors produced in the litter of any given dog that were the other than his color. It might even be that some of his or her litter mates were parti-colored. The pedigree would not show this. Of course a pedigree similar to that issued by the Verein für Deutsche Shäferhunde (German Shepherd Dog Club) in Germany, could be issued. These pedigree papers give a full history of the dog and its ancestors, listing the dogs in the litters of the animals shown on the pedigree. A similar pedigree for Poodles could be made with the colors of the litter mates of the dogs whose names appear on the pedigree.

Chapter 6
Feeding Your Poodle

Your Poodle is a carnivore, a flesh eater. His teeth are not made for grinding as are human teeth, but are chiefly fashioned for tearing and severing. Over a period of years this fact has led to the erroneous conclusion that the dog must be fed mostly on muscle meat in order to prosper. Wolves, jackals, wild dogs and foxes comprise the family Canidae to which your dog belongs. These wild relatives of the dog stalk and run down their living food in the same manner the dog would employ if he had not become attached to man. The main prey of these predators are the various hoofed herbivorous animals, small mammals and birds of their native habitat. The carnivores consume the entire body of their prey, not just the muscle meat alone. This manner of feeding has led some zoologists to consider the dog family as omnivorous (eater of both plant and animal matter), despite their obvious physical relationship to the carnivores.

You would assume, and rightly so, that the diet which keeps these wild cousins of the dog strong, healthy and fertile could be depended upon to do the same for your Poodle. Of course, in this day and age your dog cannot live off the land. He depends upon you for sustenance, and to feed him properly you must understand what essential food values the wild carnivore derives from his kill, for this is nature's supreme lesson in nutrition.

The canine hunter first laps the blood of his victim, then tears open the stomach and eats its contents, composed of predigested vegetable matter. He feasts on liver, heart, kidneys, lungs and the fat-encrusted intestines. He crushes and consumes the bones and the marrow they contain, feeds on fatty meat and connective tissue, and finally eats the lean muscle meat. From the blood, bones, marrow, internal organs and muscle meat he has absorbed minerals and proteins. The stomach and its contents have supplied vitamins and carbohydrates. From the intestines and fatty meat he gets fats, fatty acids, vitamins and carbohydrates. Other proteins come from the ligaments and connective tissue. Hair and some indigestible parts of the intestinal contents provide enough roughage for proper laxation. From the sun he basks in and the water he drinks, he absorbs supplementary vitamins and minerals. From his kill, therefore, the carnivore acquires a well-rounded diet. To supply these same essentials to your Poodle in a form which you can easily purchase is the answer to his dietary needs.

BASIC FOODS AND SUPPLEMENTS

From the standpoint of nutrition, any substance may be considered food which can be used by an animal as a body-buiiding material, a source of energy or a regulator of body activity. From the preceding paragraphs we have learned that muscle meat alone will not fill these needs and that your dog's diet must be composed of many other food materials to provide elements necessary to his growth and health. These necessary ingredients can be found in any grocery store. There you can buy all the important natural sources of the dietary essentials listed below.

1. PROTEIN: meat, dairy products, eggs, soybeans.
2. FAT: butter, cream, oils, fatty meat, milk, cream cheese, suet.
3. CARBOHYDRATES: cereals, vegetables, confectionery syrups, honey.
4. VITAMIN A: greens, peas, beans, asparagus, broccoli, eggs, milk.
5. THIAMINE: vegetables, legumes, whole grains, eggs, muscle meats, organ meats, milk, yeast.
6. RIBOFLAVIN: green leaves, milk, *liver*, cottonseed flour or meal, egg yolk, wheat germ, yeast, beef, chicken.
7. NIACIN: milk, lean meats, liver, yeast.
8. VITAMIN D: fish that contains oil (salmon, sardine, herring, cod), fish liver oils, eggs, fortified milk.
9. ASCORBIC ACID: tomatoes, citrus fruits, raw cabbage (it has not been established that Ascorbic acid is necessary for dogs).
10. IRON, CALCIUM, AND PHOSPHORUS: milk and milk products, vegetables, eggs, soybeans, bone marrow, blood, liver, oatmeal.

The first three listed essentials complement each other and compose the basic nutritional needs. Proteins build new body tissue and are composed of amino acids, which differ in combination with the different proteins. Carbohydrates furnish the fuel for growth and energy, and fat produces heat which becomes energy and enables the dog to store energy against emergency. Vitamins and minerals, in general, act as regulators of cell activity.

Maxine of Rippwood, owned by Mrs. Albert H. Greene.
Photo by Evelyn Shafer.

Proteins are essentially the basis of life, for living cells are composed of protein molecules. In this connection, an interesting scientific experiment was conducted a short while ago which led to an important discovery. A young scientist attempted to duplicate the conditions which, it is assumed, prevailed upon the earth before life began. Cosmological theory indicates that the atmosphere at that time (approximately two thousand million years ago, give or take a year) would have been poisonous to all the living organisms that exist today, with the exception of certain bacteria. When the experiment had been completed, it was found that amino acids had formed. These chemicals are the building blocks of proteins, and proteins are the basis of life. No, science has not yet produced actual life by building proteins. It is still rather difficult to even define life, let alone manufacture it. But we can sustain and give growth to living forms by proper feeding procedures.

Ch. Alekai Marlaine, owned and bred by Alekai Kennels. Sire: Ch. Alekai Kila; dam: Ch. Davdon Captivation. This white Standard is shown winning first in the Non-Sporting group at the Cape Cod Kennel Club under judge Virgil D. Johnson, handler Wendell Sammet. Photo by Evelyn Shafer.

The main objective in combining food factors is to mix them in the various amounts necessary to procure a balanced diet. This can be done in a number of ways. The essential difference in the many good methods of feeding lies in the time it takes to prepare the food and in the end cost of the materials used. Dogs can be fed expensively and they can be fed cheaply, and in each instance they can be fed equally well.

There are various food products on the market packaged specifically for canine consumption. The quality of these foods as complete diets in themselves ranges from poor to excellent. The better *canned*, or *pudding*, foods are good but expensive for large Standard Poodles, since the moisture content is high and your dog must consume a large amount for adequate nourishment. Compact and requiring no preparation, the canned foods are fine for use at shows or when traveling—though for traveling an even better diet is biscuits, lean meat and very little water. The result is less urination and defecation, since the residue from this diet is very small. The diet is, of course, not to be fed over any extended period of time because it lacks food-value.

Biscuits can be considered as tidbits rather than food, since much of the vitamin and mineral content has been destroyed by baking. The same holds true for *kibbled* foods. They are fillers to which must be added, fat, milk, broths, meat, vegetables and vitamin and mineral supplement.

By far the most complete of the manufactured foods are the *grain foods*. In such a highly competitive business as the manufacturing and merchandising of these foods, it is essential for the manufacturer to market a highly palatable and balanced ration. The better grain foods have constantly changing formulas to conform to the most recent results of scientific dietary research. They are, in many cases, the direct result of controlled generation tests in scientific kennels where their efficacy can be ascertained. A good grain food

Ch. Puttencove Brigadier, owned by Mrs. Angela M. Olcott. He is shown winning best of variety at the Devon Dog Show Association under breeder-judge Dr. Donald Davidson. Photo by Evelyn Shafer.

should not be considered merely a filler. Rather, it should be employed as the basic diet to which fillers might possibly be added. Since the grain food is bag or box packaged and not hermetically sealed, the fat content is necessarily low. A high degree of fat would produce quick rancidity. Therefore fat must be added to the dry food. Milk, which is one of the finest of foods in itself, can be added along with broths or plain warm water to arrive at the proper consistency for palatability. With such a diet we have a true balance of essentials, wastage is kept to a minimum, stools are small and firm and easily removed and cost and labor have been reduced to the smallest equation possible to arrive at and yet feed well. The *pellet type* food is simply grain food to which a binding agent has been added to hold the grains together in the desired compact form.

Fat should be introduced into the dog's diet in its pure form. Proteins and carbohydrates are converted into fat by the body. Fat also causes the dog to retain his food longer in the stomach. It stores vitamins E, K, A and D, and lessens the bulk necessary to be fed at each meal. Fat can be melted and poured over the meal, or put through the meat grinder and then mixed with the basic ration.

Just as selection is important in breeding, so ratio is important in feeding. The proper diet must not only provide all the essentials, it must also supply those essentials in the proper proportions. This is what we mean by a balanced diet. It can be dangerous to your Poodle's well being if the ratios of any of his dietary essentials are badly unbalanced over a period of time. The effects can be disastrous in the case of puppies. This is the basic rason for putting your faith in a good scientifically balanced grain dog food.

There is an abundance of concentrated *vitamin supplements* on the market specifically manufactured for dogs. They are undoubtedly of real worth—if your dog needs a supplement. Dogs fed a balanced diet do not need additional concentrated supplements, with the exception, perhaps, of the rare individual. If you feel that your dog is in need of a supplement, it is wiser to consult your veterinarian for advice and specific dosage. Check the label of the dog food you buy to make sure that it has all the necessary ingredients. If it has, you will not find it necessary to pour in concentrated, highly expensive supplements. Another of the supplements widely in use today, packaged under various trade names, embodies the elements of what was initially called A.P.F., or animal protein factor. This is a

Ch. Puttencove Moonshine, owned by Puttencove Kennels. This white Standard was best in show at the Poodle Club of America specialty. He is shown with his handler, the late Robert Gorman. Photo by Evelyn Shafer.

powder combining various antibiotic residues with the composite vitamin B_{12}. The role of this supplement in dog feeding has not, as yet, been adequately established. Theoretically, it is supposed that this supplement produces better food utilization and the production of extra body fat, which accounts for better growth and weight. On the other hand, it is also thought that it can affect the normal balance of intestinal flora, and overdoses can produce undesirable effects. Nature is generally generous in her gift of vitamins, minerals and other nutritional essentials, and all can be found, in adequate abundance, in the balanced diet. We do not want to rule out supplements, but we do want to stress that they should be used with care.

In many instances kennel owners feel that their animals, for various reasons, need a supplementary boost in their diet. Some are in critical stages of growth, bitches are about to be bred or are in whelp, mature dogs are being frequently used for stud, and others are recuperating from illness. In such cases supplements can be added to the food, but in reasonable amounts.

Calcium and *phosphorus* in pure chemical form must be handled with care when used in the dog's diet. Toxic conditions can be caused by an overabundance of this material in the bloodstream. Green, ground, edible bone meal is a much better product to use where it is thought necessary. Most good grain foods have an abundance of this inexpensive element in correct balance. Milk is a highly desirable vehicle for balanced calcium and phosphorus as well as many other nutritional needs.

Cod liver oil is another product that, if given to excess over a period of time, can cause toxicity and bone malformation. It is better and cheaper to employ a fish liver oil concentrate such as percomorph oil. In this oil the base vehicle has been discarded and the pure oil concentrated, so that a very small dosage is required. Many owners and breeders pour cod liver oil and throw handfuls of calcium and supplementary concentrates into the food pans in such lavish amounts that there is a greater bulk of these than of the basic food, on the theory that, if a little does some good, a greater amount will be of immense benefit. This concept is both ridiculous and dangerous.

An occasional pinch of *bicarbonate of soda* in the food helps to neutralize stomach acidity and can prevent, or alleviate, fatigue caused by a highly acid diet. Bones need never be fed to dogs for food value if the diet is complete. Poultry bones should never be fed. They splinter into sharp shards which can injure gums or rip the throat lining or stomach. Once in the stomach they are dissolved by strong gastric juices. It is on their way to their ultimate goal that they do damage. The same is also true of fishbones. Dogs like to chew. At pet retail counters today are many kinds of products which were manufactured to give your Poodle this natural pleasure. These products are advantageous in that they help to clean the animal's teeth, ridding them of tartar and other germ-bearing residues. These products can be considered the dog's toothbrush.

Table scraps are not recommended. A dog fed on table scraps will certainly be receiving an unbalanced and an inadequate diet. If used, they should be considered as a minor supplement to be mixed with your Poodle's scientifically prepared commercial food. Fish is a good food, containing all the food elements which are found in meat, with a bonus of extra nutritional values. *Muscle meat* lacks many essentials and is so low in calcium that, even when supplemented with vitamin D, there is grave danger of rickets developing. In its raw state, meat is frequently the intermediate host of several forms of internal parasites. Meat by-products and canned meat, which generally contains by-products, are much better as foods for dogs than pure muscle meat. Incidentally, whale meat, which is over 80 percent protein, could well replace horse meat, which is less than 50 percent protein, in the dog's diet.

Water is one of the elementary nutritional essentials. Considering the fact that the dog's body is approximately 70 percent water, which is distributed in varying percentages throughout the body tissues and organs, including the teeth and bones, it isn't difficult to realize the importance of this staple to the dog's well being. Water flushes the system, stimulates gastric juice activity, brings about better appetite, and acts as a solvent within the body. It is one of the major sources of necessary minerals and helps during hot weather, and to a lesser degree during winter, to regulate the dog's temperature. When a dog is kept from water for any appreciable length of time, dehydration occurs. This is a serious condition, a fact which is known to any dog owner whose animal has been affected by diarrhea, continuous nausea, or any of the diseases in which this form of body shrinkage occurs.

Ch. De Caplette Tar of Roblyn, owned by Anna B. Caplette and bred by Mary Dell Reese. Sire: Ch. Tar Bαby of Whitehall; dam: De Caplette Marybelle. This black Toy is seen winning best in show at the Cape Cod Kennel Club under the late Anton Korbel, handler Anne Rogers Clark. Photo by Evelyn Shafer.

Water is the cheapest part of your dog's diet, so supply it freely, particularly in warm weather. In winter, if snow and ice are present and available to your Poodle, water is not so essential. At any rate, if left in a bucket in his run, it quickly turns to ice. Yet even under these conditions it is an easy matter to bring your dog in and supply him with at least one good drink of fresh water during the day. Being so easily provided, so inexpensive, and so highly essential to your Poodle's health, sober thought dictates that we should allow our dogs to "take to drink."

Breeders with only a few dogs can sometimes afford the extra time, expense and care necessary to feed a varied and complicated diet. But it is easy to see that to feed a large kennel in such fashion would take an immense amount of time, labor and expense. Actually, the feeding of a scientifically balanced grain food as the basic diet eliminates the element of chance which exists in diets prepared by the kennel owner from natural sources, since overabundance of some specific elements, as well as a lack of others, can bring about dietary ills and deficiencies.

Caloric requirements vary with age, temperament, changes in temperature and activity. If your dog is nervous, very active, young and kept out-of-doors in winter, his caloric intake must be greater than the phlegmatic, underactive, fully grown dog who has his bed in the house. Keep your dog in good flesh, neither too fat nor too thin. You are the best judge of the amount to feed to keep him in his best condition. A well-fed Poodle should always be in show "bloom"—clear-eyed, dense-coated, filled with vim and vigor and with enough of a thin, all-over layer of fat to give him sleekness without plumpness.

To keep your Poodle's ears from becoming saturated with food or water use feeding bowls that are just wide enough to accommodate

Ch. Round Tables Cognac, owned and bred by Round Table Kennels. Sire: Ch. Round Table Conte Blanc; dam: Surrey Dancer of Round Table. This Miniature is a frequent best in show winner and is seen scoring best of variety at the International Kennel Club of Chicago under judge Henry Stoecker. Included in Cognac's impressive list of top wins is a first in the Non-Sporting group at the Westminster Kennel Club in 1966. He is presented in the ring by John J. Brennan. Photo by Evelyn Shafer.

the dog's muzzle, or tie the ears in a net and pull them back at feeding time. If the ears become messy with food or liquids, the Poodle will lick at them and ruin the coat on the ears and it will take up to a year to replace the hair lost. This could mean that a good show dog that is "hot" and winning could lose that competitive edge by being withdrawn from competition while the ear leather becomes fully coated again.

FEEDING TECHNIQUES

The consistency of the food mix can vary according to your Poodle's taste. It is best not to serve the food in too sloppy a mixture, except in the case of very young puppies. It is also good practice to feed the same basic ration at every meal so that the taste of the food does not vary greatly at each feeding. Constant changing of the diet, with supplementary meals of raw or cooked meat, tends to produce finicky eaters, the bane of the kennel and private owner's existence. Never leave the food pan before your dog for more than 30 minutes. If he hasn't eaten by then, or has merely nibbled, the pan should be removed and not presented to him again until his next feeding time. This same policy should be followed when breaking a dog to a new diet. If he has become a canine gourmet, spoiled by a delicate diet, he may sometimes refuse to eat for two or three days. But eventually, when his hunger becomes acute enough and he realizes his hunger strike will not result in coddling and the bringing forth of his former delicacies, he will eat with gusto whatever is put before him. Where there are several dogs to create mealtime competition, there is little danger of finicky eaters regardless of what is fed.

Keep your feeding utensils clean to eliminate the danger of bacterial formation and sourness, especially in warm weather. Your food pans can be of any solid metal material. Agate, porcelain, and the various types of enamel-ware have a tendency to chip, and are therefore not desirable.

Every kennel owner and breeder has his own pet diet which has proven successful in the rearing and maintenance of his stock. In each instance he will insist that his is the only worth-while diet, and he cannot be blamed for so asserting, since his particular diet has nourished and kept his own stock in top condition over a period of years. Yet the truth is, as I have mentioned before in this chapter, that there are many ways to feed dogs and feed them well, and no one diet can be said to be the best.

Perhaps it would be enlightening to the reader to explain how the dogs are fed by two small breeders, as well as the feeding procedure used in a much larger kennel. The results of these three different diets have all been excellent. There have been no runts, the growth factor in each instance has been entirely adequate, and none of the animals bred or raised have shown any signs of nutritional lack. All the dogs raised on these diets have developed normally into the full flower of their genetic inheritance, with lustrous coats, fine teeth and bones, and all possessing great vigor and stamina. Incidentally, what has been written in this chapter is applicable mostly to grown dogs, though the three feeding formulas to follow include puppy feeding as well. A more comprehensive study of puppy feeding will be found in the chapter dealing specifically with puppies.

Rogers' The Ravens Wing, owned by Betty Rogers. He is seen going best of winners at the Santa Barbara Kennel Club under Mrs. M. G. Chisholm, handler Bob Zayac. Photo by Henry C. Schley.

Diet Number 1

This diet is employed by a small Standard Poodle kennel. Dietol, an oil product, is given the pups in the nest on the second day after whelping, two drops to each puppy. The amount is gradually increased, until the second week each pup is receiving ten drops of the oil. The third week, twenty drops are given, and this is continued until a full pint has been consumed.

At 12 to 14 days, for a litter of six puppies, a cereal is cooked with one-eighth of a pound of butter or margarine, or a good special puppy meal is substituted for the cereal. To this is added one-half a can of evaporated milk, two poached eggs, cow's milk and two tablespoonsful of Karo syrup. This is fed twice daily to supplement dam's feedings.

At three weeks, the same diet is given three times a day.

At four weeks, the same diet, given four times a day. At this time, chopped beef, rich in fat, is added, and two eggs are cooked in with the cereal.

Ch. Lime Crest Topper, owned and handled by Mrs. Robert D. Levy. Topper is shown winning first in the Toy group under judge Charles A. Swartz at the Clearwater Kennel Club. Photo by Evelyn Shafer.

Between the fifth and sixth weeks the puppies are weaned. During this period, two feedings are the same as the diet fed during the fourth week, and two other feedings are composed of a good grain dog meal, moistened with broth or soup, to which has been added a heaping handful of chopped beef which is at least 25 percent fat. This food mixture is supplemented by three tablespoons of refined cod liver oil and a heaping tablespoon of a mixture of bone meal, soybean meal, brewer's yeast and a small amount of salt.

Three meals are fed as described above at three months and continued until the pups have reached the age of five months, the only variation being the use of small kibbles occasionally replacing the basic cereal or meal at two of the meals.

From five months until 12 to 14 months, two large meals are given, one in the morning and one at night, using the same diet as above, augmented by periodic table scraps.

From 14 months on the dog is fed once daily in the summer. In fall and winter the diet consists of a light breakfast of warm cereal, milk and Karo syrup. The main evening meal is composed of grain meal, or occasionally, kibbles or pellets, moistened in soup or warm water, a pound of ground fatty meat, one tablespoonful of cod liver oil or Dietol and a heaping tablespoon of the mixed supplement mentioned previously (bone meal soybean meal, and yeast). To this is added table scraps of every description, except fowl bones and fishbones.

During the winter months occasional stews of beef or lamb and fresh vegetables are cooked and relished by the dogs.

Diet Number 2

Dietol is given each puppy in increasing amounts as it grows, beginning with two drops for Standard puppies. This oil is rich in vitamin K, which is an essential vitamin for puppy survival.

At 16 days the pups are given their first supplementary feeding. From then on the Dietol is incorporated in their meals. A puppy grain meal is used as a base, to which is added a tablespoonful of Pelargon, a Nestle's dried milk product which has been enriched and acidified so that it more closely approaches the taste of the bitch's milk than does plain cow's milk. (Incidentally, if you've brought a puppy home who refuses to eat, try this product mixed with warm milk or sprinkled over the food mixture. In almost every instance it will do the trick.) Warmed cow's milk and about ten percent melted fat is added to the meal and Pelargon. Stir to the consistency of cream and allow them to eat all they can hold.

At three weeks the same mixture is fed three times a day.

At four weeks, the same mixture is fed four times a day. The fat content is raised to about 15 percent. The consistency of the food is slightly thickened, and a natural supplement, composed of alfalfa leaf meal, irradiated yeast, and ground bone meal, is added sparingly. The ratios of these ingredients, mixed together in a large jar for continued use are: two tablespoonsful of alfalfa leaf meal to one tablespoonful of yeast and three-quarters of a tablespoonful of bone meal.

At six weeks the pups are completely weaned and fed five times daily. Four of the meals are the same mixture as used at four weeks, with a small amount of canned horse meat added for taste and a scent appeal. The meals are increased in size with the growth of the pups. The last meal, the fifth at night, consists of warmed milk, half natural cow and half evaporated. After eight weeks the Pelargon is discontinued and powdered milk is used instead.

Five feedings are given until three months. Four feedings from then up to five months.

From five months until eight months, three feedings are given, eliminating the late evening milk meal. The dog is switched then from the puppy meal to a regular grain meal. Milk is added to all other meals in powder or liquid form.

Two meals from eight to eighteen months are fed and thereafter one meal, unless, as is generally the case, the individual thrives better on two meals.

Table scraps of all kinds are used, exclusive of fowl bones and fishbones. The schedule as outlined above is not necessarily a rigid one. Fish, stews, eggs (yolks only if raw, whole egg if cooked), liver and a host of other foods are occasionally incorporated into the diet. But this is the one main day in, day out diet.

Diet Number 3

This diet is used in a large kennel of hunting hounds of Standard Poodle size. During the hunting season they are hunted extensively, running miles and miles of woodland nightly, trailing their quarry. Bitches are bred regularly, whelping large litters of healthy pups.

At 16 to 18 days supplementary feeding is begun, consisting of a puppy meal and warmed evaporated milk. This mixture (of creamy consistency) is fed three times a day.

At seven weeks the puppies are completely weaned and receive four feedings daily as described above. Fat is now added to the diet to the amount of 20 percent of the dry weight of the complete ration.

This amount of fat is incorporated into the diet until the puppies are three to four months old. At this time the pups are changed to a tested adult grain meal and the fat incorporated raised to 25 percent of the dry total. The puppies are then fed twice daily, with hot water replacing the milk, until fully grown.

With full growth, only one daily feeding is given, consisting of the same diet as above.

Breeders of only a few dogs can generally spare the extra time, expense and care necessary to feed varied and complicated diets, but to feed a kennel of many dogs on complicated diets would take an immense amount of time and labor, not to mention expense, and is therefore not feasible.

Remember always that feeding ranks next to breeding in the influence it exerts on the growing dog. Knowledgeable breeding can produce genetically fine specimens, selection can improve the strain and the breed, but, without full and proper nourishment, particularly over the period of growth, the dog cannot attain to the promise of his heritage. The brusque slogan of a famous cattle breeder might well be adopted by breeders of Poodles. The motto is, "Breed, feed, weed."

Chapter 7
General Poodle Care

When you own a dog, you own a dependent. Whatever pleasure one gets out of life must be paid for in some kind of coin, and this is as applicable to the pleasure we derive from our dogs as it is in all things. With our dogs we pay the toll of constant care. This Poodle which you have taken into your home and made a part of your family life depends completely upon you for his every need. In return for the care you give him, he repays you with a special brand of love and devotion that can't be duplicated. This is the bargain you make with your dog: your care on one side of the scale, his complete idolatry on the other. Not quite a fair bargain, but we humans, unlike our dogs, are seldom completely fair and unselfish.

Good husbandry pays off in dollars and cents too, particularly if you have more than one or two dogs, or run a show and breeding kennel. Clean, well-cared for dogs are most often healthy dogs, free from parasitic invaders and the small ills that bring other and greater woes in their wake. Good feeding and proper exercise help build strength and resistance to disease, and a sizable run keeps your canine friend from wandering into the path of some speeding car. Veterinarian bills and nursing time are substantially reduced, saving you money and time, when your dog is properly cared for.

Cleanliness, that partner to labor which is owned by some to be next toGodliness, is the first essential of good dog care. This applies to the dog's surrounding environment as well as to the dog himself. If your Poodle sleeps in the house, provide him with a draft-free spot for his bed, away from general household traffic. This bed will be a well-padded dog mattress. It doesn't particularly matter what material is used, as long as it is kept clean and put in the proper place.

Feeding has been comprehensively discussed in the previous chapter, but the utensils used and the methods of feeding come more specifically under the heading of general care, so we will repeat these few facts mentioned in the previous chapter. Heavy aluminum feeding pans are best, since they are easily cleaned and do not chip as does agate or porcelain. Feed your dog regularly in the same place and at the same time. Establish a friendly and quiet atmosphere during feeding periods and do not coax him to eat. If he refuses the food or nibbles at it sparingly, remove his food and do not feed again until the next feeding period. Never allow a pan of food to stand before a healthy dog for more than 30 minutes under any circumstance. Should your Poodle's appetite continue to be off, consult your veterinarian for the cause.

If your are feeding several dogs in an outside kennel, it is good practice to remain until all are finished, observing their appetites and eating habits while you wait. Often two dogs, kenneled together and given the same amount and kind of food, show different results.

Ch. Rogers' Little Boy, owned by Betty Rogers. A black Toy, he is shown going winners dog at the Santa Barbara Kennel Club under Mrs. M. G. Chisholm enroute to his championship. He was shown by Bob Zayac. Photo by Henry C. Schley.

One will appear thin and the other in good condition. Sometimes the reason is a physiological one, but more often observation will show that the thinner dog is a slower eater than his kennel mate, that the latter dog gulps down his own food and then drives the thin dog away from his food pan before his ration is fully consumed and finishes this extra portion, too.

Never, never, force feed a healthy dog simply because he refuses an occasional meal. Force feeding and coaxing make finicky eaters and a finicky feeder is never in good coat or condition and turns feeding time into the most exasperating experience of the day. Rather than forcing or coaxing, it is better to starve your dog, showing no sympathy at all when he refuses food. If he is healthy, he will soon realize that he will experience hunger unless he eats when the food pan is put before him. He will soon develop a normal and healthy appetite. Immediately upon removing the food pans, they should be thoroughly washed and stacked, ready for the next mealtime.

During hot weather, be certain that your Poodle has a constant supply of fresh, clean water. In winter, water left outside in runs will freeze solid and be of no use to the dogs, so it is best to provide fresh water two or three times a day and remove the pail after the dogs have had their fill. Always provide water within an hour after feeding.

It has been the experience of most dog people that animals kept or kenneled outdoors, both winter and summer, are healthier and in better condition generally than their softer living housedog brethren. Light and the seasons have a great deal to do with shedding and coat condition. The outdoor dog, living in an environment approaching the natural, has regular shedding periods, after which his new coat comes in strong and dense. Housedogs living in conditions of artificial light and heat seldom possess the good coat exhibited by the dog who lives outdoors. The housedog is influenced much more by quick changes in temperature, particularly in the winter when he is brought from a warm, furnace-heated house, into the frigid out-of-doors.

PLANNING YOUR RUN

Even the housedog should be provided with an outside run and house, a domain of his own to keep him in the sun and air and protect him from disturbance by children or other dogs. There, in his run,

Arcady Black Jack, owned by Gloria C. Berlin and Mrs. Robert Wellens.
Photo by Evelyn Shafer.

he is safe from accident, and you know he can't run away to become lost, strayed or stolen. There, also, you can be sure he is not soiling or digging in your neighbor's newly planted lawn, a situation which can strain, to put it mildly, any "good-neighbor policy." Provide shade in some section of the run against the hot summer sun. Natural shade from trees is the ideal, of course, but artificial shade can be provided by a canvas overthrow placed strategically.

If you are building a kennel of several runs, remember that the length is more important than the width, and connecting runs in a row can be cut down in width if the length provided is ample.

The best surface for your run is a question open for argument. Some breeders prefer packed-down fine cinders for their run surface, claiming that this material provides good drainage and is the best surface for a dog's feet, keeping them compact and strong. Actually, heredity, and to a lesser degree, diet, are the prime factors that produce good feet in dogs, but a dog's feet will spread and lose compactness if he is kept constantly on a soft or muddy surface. Cinders do make an excellent run, but this surface also makes an admirable place in which parasite eggs and larvae can exist and thrive, and they are almost impossible to clean out from such a surface, short of resorting to a blowtorch. Cement runs are easy to clean and present a good appearance. But again, we have a porous surface into which the minute eggs of parasites can take refuge. Only by daily scrubbing with a strong disinfectant, or periodic surface burning, can concrete runs be kept free of parasite eggs and larvae.

Gravel and plain dirt runs present the same disadvantage, plus the difficulty of efficiently gathering stools from such surfaces. Dirt

Buttonwood's Cori, owned and bred by Mrs. E. Elaine Farrington. Sire: Ch. Bric A Brac Bragabout; dam: Ch. Buttonwood's Carita. Cori is shown going winners dog at the International Kennel Club of Chicago under judge Henry Stoecker, handler William J. Trainor. Photo by Evelyn Shafer.

runs also become muddy in rainy weather and dusty in dry weather, making it necessary to change bedding often, and producing, as formerly mentioned, a deleterious effect upon the animal's feet. It would seem, then, that none of these run surfaces is the perfect answer to our problem. But there is yet another run surface which can give us better control over parasitic reinfestation. On this run we employ washed builders' sand for the surface. The dog generally defecates in a limited area, almost always at the end of his run farthest from the run door and his own house. Stools can easily be removed from the sand surface, and by digging down and removing one or two inches of sand below the stool, parasitic invaders are also removed. Fresh sand is filled into the spaces left by cleaning. The sand soon packs down and becomes a solid surface. The grains drop easily from the dog's feet and are not carried into his house to soil his bedding. This sand is not expensive, and periodically the whole surface can be removed and fresh sand brought in and leveled. An ideal run would be one with a cement base which can be washed down with disinfectants or a strong borax solution (which will destroy hookworm larvae) whenever the surface sand is completely removed and before a fresh sand surface is provided.

BUILDING YOUR RUN

If you plan to build the run yourself, you might consider the "soil-cement" surface as a base rather than true cement. Soil-cement is a subsurface employed on light-traffic airfields and many suburban roads; it is inexpensive, durable and easily built without special knowledge or equipment. First remove the sod on the area to be converted into a run, then loosen the soil to a depth of about four inches with a spade and pulverize the soil, breaking up any lumps with a rake. Scatter dry cement at the rate of two-thirds of a sack of cement to a square yard of surface and mix in thoroughly with the soil until the mixture has a floury texture. Adjust your hose to a mist spray and water the surface until the soil-cement mixture will mold under pressure, and not crumble. Follow by raking the entire mixture to full depth to assure uniform moisture, and level at the same time. Now you must work quickly, compacting the run with a tamper and then rolling with a garden roller. All this must be done within a half hour or the surface will harden while still uneven. After rolling, the surface should be smooth and even. Mist-spray again, then cover with a coating of damp sawdust or soil for a week, after which the run can be used. Remember to keep a slight slope on all run surfaces so that water can drain off without puddling. Soil-cement is also excellent for paths around, or to and from, the kennels.

CLEANING YOUR RUN

In removing stools from a run, never rake them together first. This practice tends to spread worm eggs over a greater area. Remove each stool separately, and deposit it in a container. When the run is clean, carry the container to a previously prepared pit, dump the contents and cover with a layer of dirt. Hose out the container and apply disinfectant, and the job is done with a minimum of bother. In winter, due to snow and ice, very little can be done about run sanitation. But those who live in climates which have definite and varied seasons have the consolation of knowing that worm eggs do not incubate nor do fleas develop during cold weather. Therefore, they must only do whatever is possible in run cleanliness for the sake of appearance and to keep down odors.

FENCING YOUR RUN

Fencing the run is our next problem. The ideal fencing is heavy chain link with metal supporting posts set in cement, and erected by experts. But if your pocketbook cries at such an expenditure (and the cost is not small), you can do your own fencing, cutting the cost drastically by purchasing cheaper wire, using cedar posts for supports, and girding your loins for a bit of labor. Hog wire, six-inch stay wire fencing, fox wire or 14 gauge or two-inch-mesh poultry wire all can be used. Whatever fencing you employ, be sure it is high enough to rise six feet above ground level and is of a heavy enough gauge to be substantial. A mature Standard Poodle can easily scale fencing which is less than six feet high. Dig post holes, using horizontally stretched string as a guide to keep them evenly in line, and dig them deeply enough to hold the posts securely. Leave approximately six feet of space between each post hole. Paint the section of the post which is to be buried in the hole with creosote or some other good wood preservative and set the posts in the holes. Concrete and rock, poured into the hole around the post, will provide a firm base. A horizontal top rail strengthens the run materially and will make for a better job. Brace all corners and gate posts. When your posts are in and set, borrow a wire stretcher for use in applying the wire fencing to the posts. This handy instrument can make the difference between a poor and a good job.

YOUR DOG HOUSE

The dog house can be simple or elaborate, reaching the extremes from a barrel set on cement blocks, to a miniature human dwelling, complete with shingles and windows. The best kind of house comes somewhere in between these two extremes. For Standards make sure you build the house large enough, with sleeping quarters approximately three by five feet, and three feet high at the highest point. Incorporate a front porch one and one-half to two feet deep and the five-foot width of the house. If the house is correctly situated, the porch roof offers shade from the sun and the porch itself a place to lie in rainy or snowy weather. Make the skeleton framework of two by threes, first building the two side sections, allowing six inches of extra height on the uprights for floor elevation. Incorporate the porch size in the over-all length of the side pieces and remember the back slope over the sleeping portion, which will accommodate the hinged roof.

Next build the floor frame and cover it with five-eighths-inch outdoor plywood, or tongue and groove siding. Cover the sides with the same material you use for the floor. If you allow your two-by-three-inch framing to show on the outside of the house, you will have a smooth inner surface to attach your floor platform to. Keep the floor the six inches above ground level provided by your side uprights and brace the floor by nailing six-inch pieces of two by threes under the floor and to the inside bottom of the side uprights. Frame in the door section between the porch and the sleeping quarters, framing for a door four to six inches from the floor (to hold in the bedding), 18 inches wide and two feet high. Nail your plywood, or tongue and groove siding, over this framework, of course leaving the opening for the door, and nail the same wood across the back and the porch roof, thus closing the house in all around except for the roof section over the sleeping quarters. Build this section separately, with an overlay of four inches on the two sides and the back. Attach an underneath flange of wood on both sides and the rear, in from the edges, so that the flanges will fit snugly along the three outside edges of the house proper to keep out drafts and cold. Hinge this roof section to the back edge of the porch roof and cover the entire roof part with shingles or heavy tar paper, with a separate ten-inch flap stripped along and covering the hinged edge. Paint the house (blue or blue-gray paint is said to discourage flies), and it is finished.

If you wish, you may insulate with board insulation on the inside, or double flooring can be provided with insulating paper between the layers. In cold weather a gunny sack or a piece of canvas, rug or blanket should be tacked at the top edge of the doorway to fall across the opening, thus blocking out cold air. If the house is big enough, an inside partial wall can be provided at one side of the door, essentially dividing the inner portion into a front hall with a weather-blocking partition between this hall and the sleeping quarters. If you build the house without the porch, you will find it necessary to build a separate platform on which the dog can lie outside in the sun after snow or rain. Should your ambitions embrace a full-sized kennel building with office, etc., it might be wise to investigate the prefabricated kennel buildings which are now on the market.

This house that you build, because of its size, is not an easy thing to handle or carry, so we suggest that you build it as close to the site you have picked for it as possible. The site should be at the narrow end of the run, with just a few inches of the arch jutting into the run and the greater bulk of the house outside of the run proper. Situate the house at the door end of the run, so that when you approach the run, the dog will not track through his excreta, which will be distributed at the end of the run farthest from the door. Try to set the house with its side to the north and back to the west. This gives protection from the coldest compass point in winter and shades the porch in summer from the hot afternoon sun.

A house built to the dimensions advised will accommodate two or three fully grown, large Standards. Grade to the size down proportionately for your Miniatures. Toys, of course, are generally not left in an outside house. Remember that the smaller and lower you can build your house without cramping your dog (assuming that you don't live in a tropical or semi-tropical area), the warmer it will be in the winter. If the house is not too large, is well built and the doorway blocked adequately, you will be surprised by the amount of heat the dog's body will generate in cold weather to keep his sleeping quarters warm. To house several dogs, the necessary number of houses can be built or, if you wish, one house doubled in length, with a dividing partition and two doorways, to service two separate runs.

Also on the market today are several types of ready-built dog houses. These come in various sizes, and one to accommodate a Poodle can readily be purchased.

Bedding for the sleeping box can consist of marsh grass, oat, rye or wheat straw, or wood, pine or cedar shavings. The latter is said to discourage fleas and lice and possesses an aromatic odor. If any of the other materials are used, shake a liberal supply of flea powder in the bedding once a week or each time the bedding is changed. The bedding may be changed once a month, but should be changed more often in rainy or muddy weather. Old bedding should be burned so it will not become a breeding place for parasites. Periodically the dog house should be cleaned out, washed with soap and water and a good disinfectant and aired with the hinged roof section propped open.

All Poodles, whether they be pets or show dogs, require regular, daily grooming in order to look their best and to keep their coats in proper condition. A little attention paid to the coat daily will keep it from becoming disorderly and out of shape. Photo by Louise Van der Meid.

GROOMING

Grooming should be a pleasant experience and a time of silent and delightful communication between you and your dog. Try to find the time to groom your Poodle once every day. By removing dead hair, dust and skin scales in the daily grooming, you keep your dog's coat and appearance neat. This kind of daily grooming also eliminates the necessity of frequent bathings. For ordinary grooming use a comb. The comb size and closeness of teeth depend a great deal upon the size of your Poodle. For general use the teeth should be about one inch long and support about twelve teeth to the comb inch. A Resco comb (Resco is the brand name), is one of the best for the teeth do not bend even with hard usage. Your petshop can supply you with any equipment you might need. Be sure your comb is dry before you put it away. A wet comb will rust.

A good quality stiff brush and a grooming glove, the latter containing built-in wire bristles on the palm side, are useful but not entirely necessary. The Poodle's coat lends itself primarily to combing rather than brushing as it is trained and combed away from the body to stand up and fluff to its full length.

BATHING

You may bathe your dog or puppy any time you think it necessary, as long as you do not think it is necessary too frequently. Be careful in chilly weather to bathe him in a warm room and make sure he is completely dry before you allow him to venture out into the cold outdoors. When you bathe your dog, you soak him down to the skin and remove the protective oils from his coat. When a dog is exposed to rain and snow, the dampness is shed by the outer coat. Therefore he is not likely to be affected by natural seasonal conditions. Be careful, however, that he is not exposed to these same conditions directly after a bath, as there is danger of his contracting a cold. During the time of shedding, a bath once a week is not too often if the weather is warm. It helps to remove loose hair and skin scales, as does the grooming that should follow the bath when the dog is completely dry. The easiest way to insure the removal of deep dirt and odors caused by accumulated sebum is by employing a chemicalized liquid soap with a coconut-oil base. Some commercial dog soaps contain vermin poisons, but an occasional prepared vermicidal dip, after bathing and rinsing, is more effective and very much worthwhile. When bathing, rub the lather in strongly down to the skin, being careful not to get soap in the dog's eyes. Cover every inch of him with heavy lather, rub it in, scrape the excess off with your hands, rinse and dry thoroughly, then use a hand dryer or a drying cage until he is ready for grooming. There are paste soaps available that require no rinsing, making the bathing of your Poodle that much easier, or you may wish to use liquid detergents manufactured specifically for canine bathing. Prepared canned lathers, as well as dry shampoos, are all available at petshops and are all useful in keeping your Poodle clean and odorless.

If your dog has walked in tar which you find you cannot remove by bathing, you can remove it with kerosene. The kerosene should be quickly removed with strong soap and water if it is not to burn and irritate the skin. Paint can be washed off with turpentine, which must also be quickly removed for the same reasons. Some synthetic paints, varnishes, enamels and other like preparations, which are thinned with alcohol, can be removed by the same vehicle. If the paint (oil base) is close to the skin, linseed oil will dissolve it without irritation. Should your dog engage in a tête-à-tête with a skunk, wash him immediately (if you can get near him) with soap and hot water, or soak him with tomato juice if you can find enough available, then walk him in the hot sun. The odor evaporates most quickly under heat.

A box of small sticks with cotton-tipped ends, which are manufactured under various brand names, are excellent for cleaning your Poodle's ears. Drop into the ear a mixture of ether and alcohol, or of propylene glycol, to dissolve dirt and wax, then swab the ear clean with the cotton-tipped stick. Surplus liquid will quickly evaporate.

CARE OF CLAWS AND TEETH

Keep your Poodle's claws trimmed short. Overgrown claws cause lameness, foot ailments, spread toes and hare feet. If your dog does a great deal of walking on cement, claw growth is often kept under control naturally by wearing off on the cement surface. Some Poodles seem to possess a genetic factor for short claws which never need trimming, but the majority of our dogs need claw care. To accomplish this task with the least possible trouble, use a claw cutter specifically designed to trim canine claws and cut away only the

Care of the claws is very important to the appearance and comfort of a Poodle. The Poodle's feet should be small and tight. If the claws are allowed to go untrimmed the foot will spread and the dog's movement will be adversely affected. Photo by Louise Van der Meid.

horny dead section of the claw. If you cut too deeply, you will cause bleeding. A flashlight held under the claw will enable you to see the dark area of the blood line so you can avoid cutting into it. If you should tap the blood supply in the claw, don't be overly alarmed; simply keep the dog quiet until the severed capillaries close and the bleeding stops. Munsel's solution or a styptic pencil applied to the bleeding claw helps to hurry coagulation. After you have cut the claws, file them smooth with the use of a canine nail file. File from above with a downward, rounding stroke. If a claw has bled from trimming, do not file it for at least 24 hours.

Dog chewing articles will help prevent tartar from forming on your dog's teeth. Chewing also scrapes off tooth residue in the process, keeping his teeth clean and white. If tartar should form, it can be chipped off with the same kind of instrument your dentist uses on your teeth for that purpose, or your veterinarian can clean them efficiently and without bother to you. Check your dog's mouth every other week for broken, loose or abscessed teeth, particularly when he has passed his prime. Bad teeth must be tended by your veterinarian before they affect your dog's general health.

FLIES

During the summer months certain flies, commonly called "deer" flies, cause great discomfort, the formation of scabs, subsequent baldness, and sometimes infection. A good liquid insecticide, one of the many recently developed for fly control, should be rubbed or sprayed on the dog as often as necessary to keep these pests away. Skin-disease salve which contains sulphur and oil of turpentine as a vehicle is also efficacious against flies, particularly if D.D.T. flea powder is shaken on top of the salve, where it adheres, giving extra protection. Oil of benzoin and oil of cade, painted on, are also effective.

RATS

If rats invade the kennel area, they should be eradicated as quickly as possible. Not only are they disease carriers, but they are an affront to our more delicate senses. To get rid of them, set out small pans of dog meal near their holes every night for several nights until you have them coming to these pans to feed. Then mix Red Squill with the dog food they are being fed, eight measures of dog meal to one of Red Squill. After a single night's feeding of this poisonous mixture, you will generally rid your premises of these gray marauders. Red Squill is a drug that is nonpoisonous to all animals except rodents, so it can be used around the kennel with safety.

TRAVEL

When traveling in hot weather with your dog, never leave him in a closed car in the sun alone. Death takes its grisly toll each summer of dogs so treated. Carry his water pail and food dish with you and take care of his needs as you do your own when on the road. If you intend

Most dogs love to'travel. It is important though to make sure that your Poodle will not jump into anyone's car. This will help to keep your pet that much safer from dog thieves. Photo by Louise Van der Meid.

changing his diet to one more easily fed when traveling, begin the change a few days before your trip so he can become accustomed to it. Gaines Research Division publishes a list of approximately 3,500 hostelries across the country that will accept dogs—a handy booklet for the dog-loving traveler to have.

If you find it necessary to ship a Poodle to another section of the country, make sure the crate you use is large enough in all dimensions to keep the dog from being cramped during his journey. Check to see that there are no large openings or weak sections which might break in transit and allow the dog's limbs to project out of the crate. Consult your veterinarian or your local express agency for data on state health certificates. Supply the dog with a pan, rigidly attached to the crate, for water, and throw a few dog biscuits on the floor of the crate for the dog to gnaw on during his journey to alleviate boredom. Be sure there are air holes in strategic locations to provide air and ventilation. If possible, the top surface of the crate should be rounded, rather than flat, to discourage the parking of other crates on top of the dog crate. Strips of wood, nailed horizontally along the outside of the crate and projecting out from the surface will, prevent adjacent crates, or boxes, from being jammed tightly against the dog crate and thus blocking and defeating the purpose of the ventilation holes.

A periodic health check of your Poodle by your veterinarian can pay big mental and monetary dividends. When you take him for his examination, remember to bring with you samples of his stool and urine for analysis.

EXERCISE

Exercise is one of the facets of canine care that is many times neglected by the owner. Dogs need a great deal more exercise than humans, so taking your dog for a walk on leash cannot be considered exercise from the canine standpoint. If you can allow him to run free when you take him out, he will get more exercise, but still just a bare modicum of what is necessary. If you teach him to chase a ball and retrieve it, he will get still more exercise, while you can take your ease. Chasing a ball or a thrown stick is, incidentally, a very good way to exercise your dog. If you are an enthusiastic cyclist, or even if you are not terribly enthusiastic but know how to cycle, you might train your Poodle to trot along beside a bicycle. This type of exercise is excellent and will give your Poodle admirable co-ordination, muscular fluidity and tightness. Begin this kind of exercise when the dog is seven months old, if a Standard, and six months if a Miniature. A Toy, of course, is not exercised in this manner, and it is not necessary either for a Miniature. But a big Standard can get a good deal out of this exercise.

We have considered in this chapter the elements of physical care, but we must not forget that your Poodle needs mental care as well. His character and mental health need nourishment, grooming and exercise, just as much as his physical being. Give him your companionship and understanding, teach him right from wrong and treat him as you would a friend whom you enjoy associating with. This, too, is a part of his general care, and perhaps the most important part for both you and your Poodle.

Remember that good general care is the first and most important part of canine ownership and disease prevention. The health and happiness of your dog is in your hands. A small amount of labor each day by those hands is your dog's health and life insurance, and the premium is paid by your Poodle in love and devotion.

Chapter 8
The Poodle Brood Bitch

If we want to succeed in improvement within the breed, we must have an even greater trueness to breed type in our bitches than we have in their breeding partners. The productive value of the bitch is comparatively limited in scope by seasonal vagary and this, in turn, increases the importance of every litter she produces.

To begin breeding we must, of necessity, begin with a bitch as the foundation. The foundation of all things must be strong and free from faults, or the structure we build upon it will crumble. The bitch we choose for our foundation bitch must, then, be a good bitch, as fine as we can possibly acquire, not in structure alone, but

The good-producing brood bitch is always the cornerstone of a breeding program. She herself need not be a winner, but if her bloodlines are right she can be invaluable for the quality of her puppies. Photo by Three Lions.

in mentality and character as well. She is a product of her germ plasm, and this most important facet of her being must be closely analyzed so that we can compensate, in breeding, for her hidden faults. Structurally, the good brood bitch should be strongly made and up to standard size. She should be deep and not too long in body, for overlong bitches are generally too long in loin and weak in back, and after a litter tend to sag in back line. She must possess good bone strength throughout, yet she should not be so coarse as to lack femininity.

Your bitch will first come in season when she is between eight and twelve months of age. Though this is an indication that nature considers her old enough and developed enough to breed, it is best to allow her to pass this first heat and plan to breed her when she next comes in season. This should come within six months if her environment remains the same. Daylight, which is thought to affect certain glands, seems to occasionally influence the ratio of time between heats, as will complete change in environment. Scientific studies of the incidence of seasonal variation in the mating cycles of bitches indicate that more bitches come in heat and are bred during the months of February through May than at any other time of year. The figures might not be completely reliable, since they were assembled through birth registrations in the A.K.C., and many breeders refrain from fall and winter breedings so they will not have winter or early spring litters. Miniatures and Toys reach maturity much earlier than do Standards, and bitches of these varieties can be bred at first heat, which generally comes at a younger age.

In Europe, a bitch is not bred until she has passed two seasons, but it is not necessary to wait this long. In fact, should you breed your bitch at her second season, it will probably be better for her, settling her in temperament and giving her body greater maturity and grace.

When your bitch is approaching her period of heat and you intend to breed her, have her stool checked for intestinal parasites, and if any are present, have her wormed. Feed her a well-balanced diet, such as she should have been getting all along. Her appetite will increase in the preparatory stage of the mating cycle as her vulva begins to swell. She will become restless, will urinate more frequently and will allow dogs to approach her, but will not allow copulation. Within the bitch other changes are taking place at this stage. Con-

Ch. J. C. Midnight Madman, owned by Eileen M. Slyder. This black Toy was best of variety at the Cavalier Poodle Club under judge Reginald Sparkes, handler Tom Crowe. Photo by Evelyn Shafer.

gestation begins in the reproductive tract, and the horns of the uterus and the vagina thicken.

The first sign of blood from the vulva ushers in the second stage of the mating cycle. In some bitches no blood appears at all, or so little that it goes unnoticed by the owner, and sometimes we find a bitch who will bleed throughout the cycle. In either circumstance we must depend upon other signs. The bitch becomes very playful with animals of her own and the opposite sex, but will still not permit copulation. This is, of course, a condition which is very trying to male dogs with which she comes in contact. Congestion within the bitch reaches a high point during this period. Ova develop within the follicles of the ovaries, and, normally, the red discharge gradually turns to pink, becoming lighter in color until it becomes straw color and is no longer obvious. Her vulva is more swollen, and she becomes increasingly more playful with males. This period is generally of about ten days' duration, but the time varies greatly with the individual. Rather than rely upon any set time period, it is best to conclude that this period reaches its conclusion when the bitch will stand for the stud and permit copulation. This generally occurs at about the tenth day, but can take place as early as the fourth or fifth day of this period or as late as the 17th day.

The third period in the cycle is the acceptance period. The bitch will swing her hind end toward the dog, and she will permit copulation. Sometimes the stud may have to tease her for a time, but she will eventually give in. The bitch may be sensitive and yelp and pull away when the stud's penis touches the lining of the vagina. If this occurs several times, it is best to wait another day, until the sensitivity

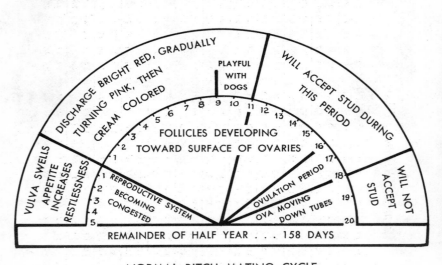

NORMAL BITCH MATING CYCLE.

has left this region. A very definite indication that the bitch is in the acceptance period is the softness and flaccidity of the vulva, from which the firmness and congestion has gone. Within the bitch the ovarian follicles have been growing ever bigger, and approximately midway in the acceptance period some of them burst and the eggs are ready for fertilization. If the bitch has a normal mating cycle, as shown on the diagram, the best time to breed her is about the thirteenth or fourteenth day of the mating cycle, when ovulation has occurred. This time also varies with the individual bitch, so that until you have bred your bitch once or twice and feel that you know the best time for her, it is better to breed her on the eleventh day and every other day thereafter until her period of acceptance is over.

Perpetual Whelping Chart

	1	2	3	4	5	6	7	8	9	10	11	12	13	14	15	16	17	18	19	20	21	22	23	24	25	26	27	28	29	30	31
Bred—Jan.	1	2	3	4	5	6	7	8	9	10	11	12	13	14	15	16	17	18	19	20	21	22	23	24	25	26	27	28	29	30	31
Due—March	5	6	7	8	9	10	11	12	13	14	15	16	17	18	19	20	21	22	23	24	25	26	27	28	29	30	31	April 1	2	3	4
Bred—Feb.	1	2	3	4	5	6	7	8	9	10	11	12	13	14	15	16	17	18	19	20	21	22	23	24	25	26	27	28			
Due—April	5	6	7	8	9	10	11	12	13	14	15	16	17	18	19	20	21	22	23	24	25	26	27	28	29	30	May 1	2			
Bred—Mar.	1	2	3	4	5	6	7	8	9	10	11	12	13	14	15	16	17	18	19	20	21	22	23	24	25	26	27	28	29	30	31
Due—May	3	4	5	6	7	8	9	10	11	12	13	14	15	16	17	18	19	20	21	22	23	24	25	26	27	28	29	30	31	June 1	2
Bred—Apr.	1	2	3	4	5	6	7	8	9	10	11	12	13	14	15	16	17	18	19	20	21	22	23	24	25	26	27	28	29	30	
Due—June	3	4	5	6	7	8	9	10	11	12	13	14	15	16	17	18	19	20	21	22	23	24	25	26	27	28	29	30	July 1	2	
Bred—May	1	2	3	4	5	6	7	8	9	10	11	12	13	14	15	16	17	18	19	20	21	22	23	24	25	26	27	28	29	30	31
Due—July	3	4	5	6	7	8	9	10	11	12	13	14	15	16	17	18	19	20	21	22	23	24	25	26	27	28	29	30	31	August 1	2
Bred—June	1	2	3	4	5	6	7	8	9	10	11	12	13	14	15	16	17	18	19	20	21	22	23	24	25	26	27	28	29	30	
Due—August	3	4	5	6	7	8	9	10	11	12	13	14	15	16	17	18	19	20	21	22	23	24	25	26	27	28	29	30	31	Sept. 1	
Bred—July	1	2	3	4	5	6	7	8	9	10	11	12	13	14	15	16	17	18	19	20	21	22	23	24	25	26	27	28	29	30	31
Due—September	2	3	4	5	6	7	8	9	10	11	12	13	14	15	16	17	18	19	20	21	22	23	24	25	26	27	28	29	30	Oct. 1	2
Bred—Aug.	1	2	3	4	5	6	7	8	9	10	11	12	13	14	15	16	17	18	19	20	21	22	23	24	25	26	27	28	29	30	31
Due—October	3	4	5	6	7	8	9	10	11	12	13	14	15	16	17	18	19	20	21	22	23	24	25	26	27	28	29	30	31	Nov. 1	2
Bred—Sept.	1	2	3	4	5	6	7	8	9	10	11	12	13	14	15	16	17	18	19	20	21	22	23	24	25	26	27	28	29	30	
Due—November	3	4	5	6	7	8	9	10	11	12	13	14	15	16	17	18	19	20	21	22	23	24	25	26	27	28	29	30	Dec. 1	2	
Bred—Oct.	1	2	3	4	5	6	7	8	9	10	11	12	13	14	15	16	17	18	19	20	21	22	23	24	25	26	27	28	29	30	31
Due—December	3	4	5	6	7	8	9	10	11	12	13	14	15	16	17	18	19	20	21	22	23	24	25	26	27	28	29	30	31	Jan. 1	2
Bred—Nov.	1	2	3	4	5	6	7	8	9	10	11	12	13	14	15	16	17	18	19	20	21	22	23	24	25	26	27	28	29	30	
Due—January	3	4	5	6	7	8	9	10	11	12	13	14	15	16	17	18	19	20	21	22	23	24	25	26	27	28	29	30	31	Feb. 1	
Bred—Dec.	1	2	3	4	5	6	7	8	9	10	11	12	13	14	15	16	17	18	19	20	21	22	23	24	25	26	27	28	29	30	31
Due—February	2	3	4	5	6	7	8	9	10	11	12	13	14	15	16	17	18	19	20	21	22	23	24	25	26	27	28	March 1	2	3	4

This last, of course, is generally only possible when the stud is owned by you. One good breeding is actually all that is necessary to make your bitch pregnant, providing that breeding is made at the right time. If copulation is forced before the bitch is ready, the result is no conception or a small litter, since the sperm must wait for ovulation and the life of the sperm is limited. The acceptance period ceases rather abruptly, and is signaled by the bitch's definite resistance to male advances.

If your bitch is a maiden, it is best to breed her this first time to an older stud who knows his business. When you bring her to the stud and if there are adjoining wire-enclosed runs, put the stud in one run and the bitch in the adjacent one. They will make overtures through the wire and later, when the stud is loosed in the run with the bitch, copulation generally occurs quickly. You may have to hold the bitch if she is flighty or reluctant, sometimes a problem with maiden bitches. If your bitch fails to conceive from a good and proper breeding, do not immediately put the blame on the stud. In most instances it is the fault of either the bitch or the owner of the bitch, who has not adequately timed the mating. Many owners fail to recognize the first signs of the mating cycle and so bring their bitch to the stud either too early or too late. Normal physiology of the reproductive system can be interrupted or delayed by disturbance, disease or illness in any part of the dog's body. A sick bitch will therefore generally not come in season, though it is time to do so, until after she has completely recovered and returned to normal. Bitches past their prime and older tend to have a shorter mating cycle and so must be bred sooner than usual to assure pregnancy.

During copulation and the resulting tie, you should assist the stud dog owner as much as possible. If the stud evidences pain when he attempts to force his penis in the vulva, check the bitch. In virgin bitches you may find a web of flesh which runs vertically across the vaginal opening and causes pain to the dog when his penis is forced against it. This web must be broken by hooking your finger around it and pulling if a breeding is to be consummated. After the tense excitement of the breeding and while the tie is in effect, speak to the bitch quietly and keep her from moving until the tie is broken, then snap a leash onto her collar and take her for a slow walk. After that she can be taken home in the car. If it is necessary to travel any great distance before she arrives again in familiar surroundings, it is

Hall's Golden Rambler, owned by Margaret R. Hall. This promising youngster is a credit to his breeder and the bloodline from which he came. The ability to produce winners from puppyhood on is one of the great challenges and rewards of the hobby of dog breeding. Photo by Louise Van der Meid.

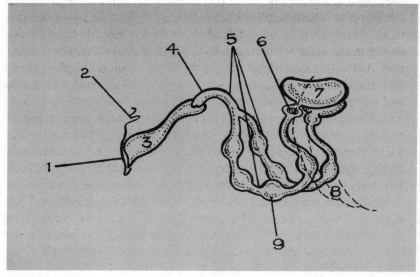

The reproductive system of the bitch: 1, vulva; 2, anus; 3, vagina; 4, cervix; 5, uterus; 6, ovary; 7, kidneys; 8, ribs; 9, fetal lump.

best to allow her a period of quiet rest before attempting the journey.

Occasionally fertile bitches, whether bred or not, will have phantom pregnancies and show every physical manifestation of true gestation up to the last moment. In some cases a bitch may be truly bred and then, after a month, resorb her fetuses. The only way of differentiating between pseudo-pregnancy and fetal resorbtion is by palpation, or feeling with the hands, to locate the fetal lump in the uterus. This is a difficult task for one who has not had vast experience.

After you have returned home with your bitch, do not allow any males near her. She can become impregnated by a second dog and whelp a litter of mixed paternity, some of the puppies sired by the first dog and others sired by the second animal. Often a bitch is bred to a selected stud just before ovulation. The sperm will live long enough to fertilize the eggs when they flush down. The next day, another male breeds to the bitch, the sperm of the two dogs mix within her and both become sires of the resulting litter.

Let us assume that your bitch is in good health and you have had a good breeding to the stud of your choice at the proper time in the bitch's mating cycle to insure pregnancy. The male sperm fertilize the eggs and life begins. From this moment on you will begin to feed the puppies which will be born in about sixty to sixty-three days from ovulation. Every bit of food you give the bitch is nutritionally aiding in the fetal development within her. Be sure that she is being provided with enough milk to supply calcium, meat for phosphorus and iron, and all the other essential vitamins and minerals. A vitamin and mineral supplement may be incorporated into the food if used moderately. Alfalfa leaf meal of 24 percent protein content should become part of the diet. She must be fed well for her own maintenance and for the development of the young *in utero*, particularly during the last 30 days of the gestation period. She should not, however, be given food to such excess that she becomes fat.

Your bitch, her run and house or bed should be free of worm and flea eggs. She should be allowed a moderate amount of free exercise in the pre-natal period to keep her from becoming fat and soft and from losing muscular tone and elasticity. If your bitch has not had enough exercise prior to breeding and you wish to harden and reduce her, accustom her to the exercise gradually and it will do her a great deal of good. But do not allow her to indulge in unaccustomed, abrupt or violent exercise, or she might abort.

The puppies develop in the horns of the uterus, not in the "tubes" (Fallopian tubes), as is commonly thought. As the puppies develop, the horns of the uterus lengthen and the walls expand until the uterus may become as long as three feet in a Standard Poodle bitch carrying a large litter. A month before the bitch is due to whelp, incorporate fresh liver in her diet two or three times a week. This helps to keep her free from constipation and aids in the coming necessary production of milk for the litter. If the litter is going to be small, she will not show much sign until late in the gestation period. But if the litter is going to be a normal or large one, she will begin to show distention of the abdomen at about 35 days after the breeding. Her appetite will have been increasing during this time, and gradually the fact of her pregnancy will become more and more evident.

Several days before she is due to whelp, the whelping box should be prepared. It should be located in a dimly lit area removed from disturbance by other dogs, or humans. The box should be about four feet square (for Standards, Miniatures and Toys proportionately smaller), enclosed on all sides by eight- to ten-inch high boards, either plank or plywood. Boards of the same height must be added

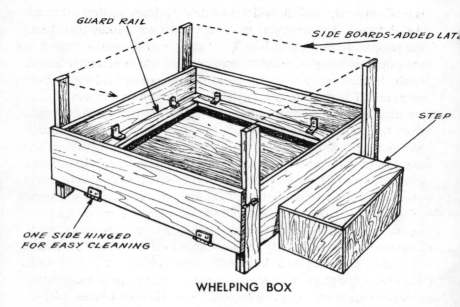

WHELPING BOX

above these in about three weeks to keep the pups from climbing out. Four inches up from the flooring (when it is packed down), a one- by three-inch smooth wooden slat should be attached to the sides with small angle irons, all around as a rail, or a pipe rail can be used. This will prevent the bitch from accidentally squeezing to death any puppy which crawls behind her. On the floor of the box lay a smooth piece of rubber matting which is easily removed and cleaned when the bedding is cleaned or changed. The bedding itself should be of rye or oat straw, and enough of it supplied so that the bitch can hollow out a nest and still leave some of the nesting material under the pups. Another method much used is to have several layers of newspapers in the bottom of the box so that they can be removed one or two at a time as they become soiled during whelping. After the litter is completely whelped, the straw bedding is provided and hollowed into a saucer shape so the whelps will be kept together in a limited area. The whelping box should be raised from the ground and a smaller box or step provided, to make it easier for the bitch to enter or leave.

As the time approaches for the whelping, the bitch will become restless; she may refuse food and begin to make her nest. Her temperature will drop approximately one degree the day before she is ready to whelp, and she will show a definite dropping down through the abdomen. Labor begins with pressure from within that forces the puppies toward the pelvis. The bitch generally twists around as the puppy is being expelled to lick the fluid which accompanies the birth. Sometimes the sac surrounding the puppy will burst from pressure. If it doesn't, the puppy will be born in the sac, a thin, membranous material called the fetal envelope. The navel cord runs from the puppy's navel to the afterbirth, or placenta. If the bitch is left alone at whelping time, she will rip the fetal caul, bite off the navel cord and eat the sac, cord and placenta. Should the cord be broken off in birth so that the placenta remains in the bitch, it will generally be expelled with the birth of the next whelp. After disposing of these items, the bitch will lick and clean the new puppy until the next one is about to be born, and the process will then repeat itself. Under completely normal circumstances, your bitch is quite able to whelp her litter and look after them without any help from you, but since the whelping might not be normal, it is best for the breeder to be present, particularly so in the case of bitches who are having their first litter.

If the breeder is present, he or she can remove the sac, cut the umbilical cord and gently pull on the rest of the cord, assuming that the placenta has not yet been ejected, until it is detached and drawn out. Some breeders keep a small box handy in which they place each placenta, so they can, when the whelping is completed, check them against the number of puppies to make sure that no placenta has been retained. The navel cord should be cut about three inches from the puppy's belly. The surplus will dry up and drop off in a few days. There is no need to tie it after cutting. You need not attempt to sterilize your hands or the implements you might use in helping the bitch to whelp, since the puppies will be practically surrounded with bacteria of all kinds, some benign and others which they are born equipped to combat.

If a bitch seems to be having difficulty in expelling a particularly large puppy, you can help by wrapping a towel around your hands to give you purchase, grasping the partly expelled whelp, and gently pulling. Do not pull hard, or you might injure the puppy. The puppies can be born either head first or tail first, head first is normal. As the pups are born, the sac broken and the cord snipped, dry them gently but vigorously with a towel and put them at the mother's breast, first squeezing some milk to the surface and then opening their mouths for the entrance of the teat. You may have to hold them there by the head until they begin sucking.

Often several puppies are born in rapid succession, then an interval of time may elapse before another one is born. If the bitch is a slow whelper and seems to be laboring hard after one or more puppies have been born, regular injections of Pitocin, at three-hour intervals, using about 1/10 c.c., can help her in delivery. Pituitrin, is a similar drug though Pitocin brings less nausea and directly affects the uterus. Both these drugs should be administered hypodermically into the hind leg of the bitch at the rear of the thigh. After the bitch has seemingly completed her whelping, it is good practice to administer another shot of the drug to make sure no last pup, alive or dead, is still unborn and to cause her to clean out any residue left from the whelping. Never use either of these drugs until she has whelped at least one puppy.

Allow her to rest quietly and enjoy the new sensation of motherhood for several hours, then insist that she leave her litter, though

All puppies should be inspected at birth to determine that all is normal with them and that no congenital deformities exist. Photo by Louise Van der Meid.

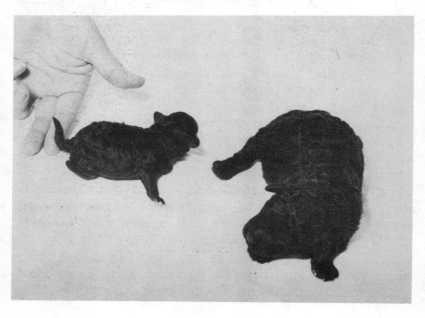

It is a good idea to weigh each whelp shortly after it is born and to continue weekly weight checks as a matter of course. In this way one can tell how satisfactorily each puppy is coming along. Photo by Louise Van der Meid.

she won't want to, and take her out to relieve herself. Offer her some warm milk. From then on, feed her as recommended during the gestation period, with the addition of three milk feedings per day. Sometimes milk appears in the udders before birth, but generally it comes in when the pups begin to nurse, since it is manufactured by glands, from blood, while the puppies are at the breast.

Now is the time to cull the litter. Of course, all young which are not normal should be culled immediately at birth. If the bitch whelps six or less pups and all seem strong and healthy, no culling is required. If she has a particularly large litter, it does not pay, in the long run, to raise all the whelps. Allow her to keep six or seven of the best and sturdiest and cull the rest. Those which you have retained will grow better and be larger and stronger than if you allowed the entire large litter to live. Quiet puppies are healthy ones. Constant crying and squirming of the puppies is a danger signal, and a check should be made to see what ails them. It may be that the bitch is not providing enough milk and they are hungry, or perhaps they are cold. Sometimes the trouble is parasitic infection, or possibly coccidiosis, or navel infection. Dr. Walter Koch, in 1950, at the University of Munich, Animal Institute, reported a bacillus, *Aerogenes*, which he claimed caused many deaths of young puppies. This bacillus infects from contact with the dam's rectum. It multiplies rapidly in the whelp's intestines, and the normal bacilli in the stomach and intestines seem to have no effect on the lethal bacillus. It begins with the first digestion of the pups and attacks the basic internal organs, exhibiting symptoms on the second or third day following birth. The puppies develop cramps, fail to suck, whimper and die within two or three days. The disease does not seem to be contagious to the other puppies. If there is something wrong with the pups, whatever it may be, you need professional advice and should call your veterinarian immediately.

Litters of Standard Poodles vary in number from 6 to 14. Miniatures generally have litters of from 3 to 5, and Toys whelp from 1 to 4 pups.

Except for the removal of dewclaws and the tail dock, the puppies, if healthy, need not be bothered until it is time to begin their supplementary feeding at about three weeks. Dewclaws should be removed on about the second day after birth. Puppies and their needs, dietary and otherwise, are discussed more fully in another chapter.

There are several ills which might befall the bitch during gestation and whelping which must be considered. Eclampsia, sometimes called milk fever, is perhaps most common. This is a metabolic disturbance brought on by a deficiency of calcium in the diet of the bitch. If you give your bitch plenty of milk and a good diet such as we have recommended, she should not be troubled with this condition. Should your bitch develop eclampsia—evidenced by troubled shaking, wild expression, muscular rigidity, and a high temperature—it can be quickly relieved by an injection of calcium gluconate into a vein.

Should your bitch be bred by accident to an undesirable animal, your veterinarian can cause her to abort by the use of any one of several efficient canine abortifacients. He can also aid old bitches who have been resorbing their fetuses to carry them full term and whelp with the aid of stilbestrol.

Mastitis, an udder infection, is a chief cause of puppy deaths. It is generally mistaken by the uninformed for "acid milk," a condition which does not exist in dogs because the bitch's milk is naturally acid. Mastitis is an udder infection which cuts off part of the milk supply and the whelps either die of infection, contracted from the infected milk, or from starvation, due to the lack of sufficient milk. It is not necessary to massage the dam's breasts at weaning time with camphorated oil. They will cake naturally and quickly quit secreting milk if left completely alone.

Growths, infections, injuries, cysts and other and various ailments can effect the female reproductive system and must be taken care of by your veterinarian. The great majority of bitches who have been well cared for and well fed are strong and healthy, and the bearing of litters is a natural procedure—the normal function of the female of the species to bear and rear the next generation, and in so doing fulfill her precious destiny.

Chapter 9
The Poodle Stud Dog

A famous breeder once wrote, "Modern breeding research has taught us that it is not so much the appearance of an animal that indicates its breeding values, but rather its hereditary picture, which means the sum total of the qualities and characteristics which it has inherited from its ancestors." This statement is as true today as when it was written in 1930, and is particularly applicable to the stud dog because of his great influence on the breed.

If what we have said before about the unrivaled importance of the brood bitch is true, it may be difficult to understand why we pay so much attention to the male lines of descent. The reason is that stud dogs tend to mold the aspects of the breed on the whole and in any given country, or locality, to a much greater extent than do brood bitches. While the brood bitch may control type in a kennel, the stud dog can control type over a much larger area. The truth of this can be ascertained by the application of simple mathematics.

Let us assume that the average litter is comprised of five puppies. The brood bitch will produce, then, a maximum of ten puppies a year. In that same year a popular, good-producing, well-publicized stud dog may be used on the average of three times weekly (many name studs, in various breeds, have been used even more frequently over a period of several years). This popular stud can sire 15 puppies a week, employing the figures mentioned above, or 780 puppies a year. Compare this total to the bitch's yearly total of ten puppies and you can readily see why any one stud dog wields a much greater influence over the breed in general than does a specific brood bitch.

The care of the stud dog follows the same procedure as outlined in the chapter on general care. He needs a balanced diet, clean quarters and plenty of exercise, but no special care as does the brood bitch. Though it is against most of the advice previously written on the subject, we recommend that the stud be used in breeding for the

Ch. Wycliffe Xavier, owned by Frank H. and Susan B. Dale and bred by Jean M. Lyle. Sire: Ch. Wycliffe Timothy; dam: Ch. Wycliffe Jacqueline. This handsome black Standard is shown winning best of variety at the Westminster Kennel Club in 1965 under judge Percy Roberts, handler Frank T. Sabella. Xavier went on to place third in the Non-Sporting group under judge Haskell Schuffman. Photo by Evelyn Shafer.

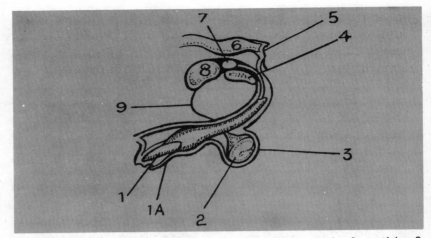

The reproductive system of a male: 1a, sheath; 1, penis; 2, testicle; 3, scrotum; 4, pelvic bone; 5, anus; 6, rectum; 7, prostate; 8, bladder; 9, vas deferens.

first time when he is about twelve months old. He is as capable of siring a litter of fine and healthy puppies at this age as he ever will be. He should be bred to a steady, knowing bitch who has been bred before, and when she is entirely ready to accept him. Aid him if necessary this first time. See that nothing disturbs him during copulation. In fact, the object of this initial breeding is to see that all goes smoothly and easily. If you succeed in this aim, the young dog will be a willing and eager stud for the rest of his life, the kind of stud that it is a pleasure to own and use.

After this first breeding, use him sparingly until he has reached 16 or 17 months of age. After that, if he is in good health, there is no reason why he cannot be used at least once a week or more during his best and most fertile years.

The male organs vital for reproduction consist of a pair each of: testicles, where the sperm is produced; epididymdes, in which the sperm are stored; and vas deferentia, through which the sperm are transported. Unlike man, the dog possesses no seminal vesicle. But, like man, the male dog is always in an active stage of reproduction and can be used at any time.

When the stud has played with the bitch for a short period and the bitch is ready, he will cover her. There is a bone in his penis, and behind this bone is a group of very sensitive nerves which cause a violent thrust reflex when pressure is applied. His penis, unlike most other animals', has a bulbous enlargement at its base. When the penis is thrust into the bitch's vagina, it goes through a muscular ring at the opening of the vagina. As it passes into the vagina, pressure on the reflex nerves causes a violent thrust forward, and the penis, and particularly the bulb, swells enormously, preventing withdrawal through the constriction band of the vulva. The stud ejaculates semen swarming with sperm, which is forced through the cervix and uterus and into the Fallopian tubes, which lie adjacent to the ovaries, and the breeding is consummated.

The dog and bitch are tied, or "hung," and the active part of the breeding is completed. The owner of the bitch should then stand at her head and hold her by the collar. The stud's owner should kneel next to the animals with his hand or knee under the bitch's stomach, directly in front of her hindquarters, to prevent her from suddenly sitting while still tied. He should talk soothingly to the stud and gently

Ch. Ledahof Silverlaine, owned by Mrs. E. A. Dalton.
Photo by Evelyn Shafer.

133

Ch. Carrillon Colin of Puttencove, shown with his owner, Mrs. George Putnam, after he was chosen best of variety at the Westminster Kennel Club in 1949. Acme Photo.

prevent him from attempting to leave the bitch for a little while. Presently the stud owner should turn the dog around off the bitch's back by first lifting the front legs off and to the ground and then lifting one hind leg over the back of the bitch until dog and bitch are standing tail to tail.

Dogs remain in this position for various lengths of time after copulation, but 15 minutes to a half an hour is generally average. When the congestion of blood leaves the penis, the bulb shrinks and the animals part.

The stud owner should keep a muzzle handy to be used on snappy bitches. Many bitches, due to temperament, environment or fright, may cause injury to the stud by biting. If she shows any indication of such conduct, she should be muzzled. Should she continue to attempt to bite for any length of time, it is generally because it is either too early or too late in the estrous cycle to consummate a breeding. If the bitch is small, sinks down when mounted or won't stand, she must be held up. In some instances her owner or the stud's owner will have to kneel next to her and, with his hand under and between her hind legs, push the vulva up toward the dog's penis or guide the stud's penis into her vulva. Straw or earth, pushed under her hind legs to elevate her rear quarters, is effective in the case of a bitch who is very much too small for the stud.

As mentioned before, many novice bitch owners fail to recognize the initial signs of the oncoming heat period, or neglect to check, so that their knowledge of elapsed time since the first showing of red is only approximate. Many offer little aid in the attempt to complete the breeding, and talk incessantly and to no purpose, generally expressing wonder at their bitch's unorthodox conduct, but do little to quiet her. In many instances, particularly with a woman, these actions are due to embarrassment. Regardless of the reason, remember to use the muzzle only on the bitch. We must always put the welfare of our dogs ahead of self.

There is not much more that can be written about the stud, except to caution the stud owner to be careful of using drugs or injections to make his dog eager to mate or more fertile. The number of puppies born in any litter is not dependent upon the healthy and fertile male's sperm, but upon the number of eggs the bitch gives off. Should your dog prove sterile, look for basic causes first. If there seems to be no physical reason for his sterility, then a series of injections by your veterinarian (perhaps of A-P-L, anterior-pituitary-like injections) might prove efficacious.

It is often a good idea to feed the dog a light meal before he is used, particularly if he is a reluctant stud. Young, or virgin, studs often regurgitate due to excitement, but it does them no harm. After the tie has broken, allow both dog and bitch to drink moderately.

Chapter 10
The Poodle Puppy

The birth of a litter has been covered in the chapter on the brood bitch. As we indicated in that discussion, barring accident or complications at birth, there is little you can do for your Poodle puppies until they are approximately three weeks old. At that age supplementary feeding begins. But suppose that for one reason or another the mother must be taken from her brood: What care must be given to these small Poodles if they are to survive? Puppies need warmth. This is provided partly by their instinctive habit of gathering together in the nest, but to a much greater extent by the warmth of the mother's body. If the mother must be taken from the nest, this extra warmth can be provided by an ordinary light bulb, or, better still, an infra-red bulb, hung directly over the brood in the enclosed nest box.

By far the most important requirement of these newborn pups is proper food. Puppies are belly and instinct, and nothing much more. They must be fed well and frequently. What shall we feed them, what formula can we arrive at that most closely approaches the natural milk of the mother, which we know is best? There are prepared modified milks for orphan puppies which are commercially available and very worth while, or you can mix your own formula of ingredients which will most closely simulate natural bitch's milk. To do this, you must first know the basic quality of the dam's milk. Bitch's milk is comparatively acid; it contains less sugar and water, more ash and protein, and far more fat than cow or human milk, so we must modify our formula to conform to these differences.

To begin, purchase a can of Nestlé's Pelargon, a spray-dried, acidified and homogenized modified milk product. If you can't get Pelargon, try any of the spray-dried baby milks, but Pelargon is best since it is, like bitches' milk, slightly acid and rich in necessary nutritive substances. To one ounce of the modified milk product,

Much of what a dog will develop into depends on the type of care he receives during the first few months of his life. The well-adjusted, happy puppy always has a far greater chance of developing into the most satisfactory pet or show dog. Photo by Louise Van der Meid.

Ch. Lemgyn's Achilles, owned by Lemgyn Kennels. A black Standard, this young winner is shown scoring a 5-point major under breeder judge Mrs. George Putnam at the Poodle Club of Southern California, handler Bob Zayac. Photo by Henry C. Schley.

add one ounce of fresh cream. Pour six ounces of water by volume into this mixture and blend with an electric mixer or egg beater until it is smooth. Larger amounts can be mixed employing the same basic proportions and kept refrigerated. This formula should be fed five or six times a day and, when fed, must be warmed to body heat. Many puppies refuse to drink a formula which has not been warmed to just the right temperature. Do not add lime water, glucose or dextrose to the formula, for by so doing you are modifying in the wrong direction. An ordinary baby's bottle and nipple are adequate as the formula vehicle. Never drop liquids directly into the puppy's throat with an eye dropper or you invite pneumonia. A twelve-ounce puppy will absorb one ounce of formula; a one-pound puppy, approximately one and three-quarter ounces of formula; a two-pound puppy, two ounces; and a three-pound puppy, two and three-

Ch. Annsown Gay Knight of Arhill, owned by Mr. and Mrs. Charles E. Wegmann. This black Standard was best in show at the Hunterdon Hills Kennel Club under the late E. H. Goodwin, handler Howard Tyler. Photo by Evelyn Shafer.

quarter ounces at each feeding. A valuable adjunct to the puppy's diet, whether formula or breast fed, is two drops of Dietol, dropped into the lip pocket from the first day of birth on, the amount to be increased with greater growth and age.

If it is possible to find a foster mother for orphan puppies, your troubles are over. Most lactating bitches will readily take to puppies other than their own if the new babies are first prepared by spreading some of the foster mother's milk over their tiny bodies. The foster mother will lick them clean and welcome them to the nest.

When the pups are two and one-half to three weeks old, the mother will often engage in an action which might prove slightly disgusting to the neophyte, but which is an instinctive and natural performance to the bitch. She will regurgitate her own stomach contents of partially digested food for her puppies to eat, thus beginning, in her own way, the weaning process. If you have begun supplementary feeding in time, this action by the bitch will seldom occur. If you haven't, it is a definite indication that supplementary feeding should begin at once.

Care should be taken when giving water to young puppies. They should get water only at certain times. Otherwise they will always have the need to urinate. Photo by Louise Van der Meid.

House training is made much easier when puppies are given access to an outdoor pen. They will come to associate the outdoors with their natural functions and so will be far more trustworthy indoors. Photo by Louise Van der Meid.

Puppies grow best on milk, meat, fat and cereal diets. Growth is attained through proteins, but proteins differ, so that puppies fed on vegetable protein diets will not grow and thrive as well as those fed animal proteins. Vitamins E and K (found in alfalfa meal) are essential to the puppies' well being and should be used in adequate amounts in the food ration. Remember that 70 percent of the puppy's energy is derived from fat intake, so supply this food element generously in the diet. Lime water should not be incorporated in the diet since it neutralizes stomach acidity, a condition which is necessary to the assimilation of fat. In experiments, puppies on fat-free diets developed deficiency symptoms characterized by anemia, weight loss, dull coats and finally, death. Fat alone could not cure the advanced manifestation of the condition, indicating that some metabolic process was disturbed when complete fat removal in the diet was resorted to. But feeding butterfat plus folacin resulted in dramatic cures.

To begin the small puppy on supplementary feeding, place the pan of food before him, gently grasp his head behind the ears, and dip his lips and chin into the food. The puppy will lick his lips, taste the food, and in no time at all learn to feed by himself. Be careful not to push the head in so far that the puppy's nose is covered and clogged by food.

141

Lemgyn's Velvet (left), owned by Lemgyn Kennels. This bitch was best of variety puppy at the Poodle Club of Southern California under Mrs. George Putnam. She was handled to this nice win by her owner, Lem Fugitt. Velvet's sire, Ch. Lemgyn's Achilles is shown (right), handled by Bob Zayac. Photo by Wentzle Ruml, III.

For the main meals (those not consisting of just milk), a Miniature puppy will need about 4 tablespoons of food, a Toy from 2 to 3, and a Standard puppy about a cup full. Miniature puppies should gain about 6 ounces a week, Toys about 3 ounces, and Standards should gain at least a pound a week. As the puppies get older the quantity of each meal is, of course, increased and the number of meals decreased.

Check the puppies' navels every day to see that infection has not set in. This infection comes from the scraping of their soft bellies on a rough surface and can generally be avoided if several thicknesses of cloth covers the floor of the nest box under the bedding.

Clip the sharp little nails to avoid damage to litter mates' eyes, which will open at about ten days. If the puppies are born with hind dew claws, cut them off with manicure scissors about two days after birth. Clip off front dew claws at the same time. They need not be bandaged, as the bitch will keep the wound clean until it has healed. Have a fecal check made when the pups are about three and one-half weeks old. If they are infested with worms, worm them immediately. Do not attempt to build up the pups first if the parasitic infestation has made them unthrifty. It is best to rid them of the worms quickly, after which they will speedily return to normal health and plumpness. On the fourth or fifth day dock the tails, exactly half length. Or, if you are a bit squeamish about dewclaws, have your veterinarian do dewclaws and tails at the same time. Poodles do not generally have dewclaws on the hind legs (hind dewclaws are the result of a simple recessive), but it is best to check for them. The front leg dewclaws must be removed in Poodles.

The weeks that fly by as the litter develops have not been wasted by the breeder. He has spent many hours in close observation of the litter and has centered his interest on one pup which he thinks shows the most promise. Either he will hold this pup for himself, sell him to a show-conscious buyer or keep the puppy and sell it at a higher price when it has become more fully developed and its early promise becomes a fact. The strange part about this whole business of picking a young puppy from a litter is that the novice buyer many times stands as good a chance of picking the best pup as the seasoned and experienced breeder. The reason for this seeming incongruity lies in the fact that in every litter there will be several pups which, if well bred and well cared for, appear to be potential winners at eight to ten weeks of age. Another reason concerns the ratio of sectional growth in young animals. Each pup, as an individual, will have a different growth rate and exhibit change in relative sections of the body, as well as in over-all growth, from day to day.

SELECTING YOUR POODLE PUPPY

If you are the potential purchaser of a Poodle puppy, or a grown dog for that matter, prepare yourself for the purchase first by attending as many shows as possible, especially breed shows where Poodle specialty judges are officiating. Observe, absorb and listen. Visit kennels which have well-bred, winning stock, and at shows and kennels make an unholy nuisance of yourself by asking innumerable questions of Poodle people who have proved, by their record in the breed, that information gleaned from them can be respected. When you intend to purchase a new car, or an electrical appliance such as a refrigerator or washing machine, you go to sales rooms and examine the different makes, weighing their features and quality, one against the other. You inquire of friends who have different brands their opinion in regard to the utility value of the item, and, when you have made up your mind which brand is best, you make sure that you purchase the item from a reliable distributor. Do the same thing when you intend to purchase a dog. Before you make your journey to buy a puppy, be sure to inquire first into the background of the seller as well as the background of his dogs. What does he actually know about this breed? What has he formerly produced? What is his reputation amongst other reputable people? Does his stock have balanced minds as well as balanced bodies? Find the answers to these questions even before you delve into the ancestry of the puppies he has for sale. If the answers prove that this person is an honest, dependable person with more than a smattering knowledge of the breed, and that he has sold consistently typical stock, then your next step will be to study the breeding of his puppies to determine whether they have been bred from worth-while stock which come from good producing strains. Examine stock he has sold from different breedings to other customers. Be careful of kennels which are puppy factories, breeding solely for commercial reasons, and don't be carried away by hysterical, overdone, adjective-happy advertisements.

When you have satisfied yourself that the seller is a morally responsible person who has good stock, then you may sally forth to purchase your future champion. It is best, if possible, to invite an experienced breeder to accompany you on your mission. As mentioned before, even the most experienced fancier cannot with assurance pick the puppy in the litter which will mature into the best specimen. An experienced person can, however, keep you from selecting a very engaging youngster which exhibits obvious faults which quite possibly won't improve.

Assuming that the litter from which you are going to select your puppy is a fat and healthy one and it is a male puppy you have set your heart on having, ask the breeder to separate the sexes, so you can examine the male puppies only. Normal puppies are friendly, lovable creatures wanting immediate attention, so the little fellow who backs away from you and runs away and hides should be eliminated from consideration immediately. This also applies to

The person that intends to buy a puppy should make it his or her business to locate a reputable breeder, and having found that individual, to make sure that the puppy that is bought is a normal, healthy, well-adjusted animal. Photo by Louise Van der Meid.

the puppy which sulks in a corner and wants no part of the proceedings. Watch the puppies from a short distance as they play and frolic, sometimes trotting and occasionally quitting their play for a fleeting moment to stand gazing at something of interest which has, for that second, engaged their attention. Don't be rushed. Take all the time necessary to pick the puppy you want. You are about to pay cold cash for a companion and a dependent who will be with you for many years.

If you have been lucky enough to have had the opportunity of examining both sire and dam, determine which puppies exhibit the faults of the parents or the strain. If any particular fault seems to be overdone in a specific puppy, discard him from further consideration. Do not handle the puppies during this preliminary

Ch. Silhou-Jette's Cream Topping, owned by Challendon Kennels.
Photo by Evelyn Shafer.

Ch. Douai Atlanta, owned by Douai Kennels. Photo by Evelyn Shafer.

examination. Look for over-all balance first and the absence of glaring structural faults.

You will probably have a definite color and size in mind and you will have, I assume, gone to a kennel that is known for this specific size. By seeing the parents you will know whether or not the puppies come from stock that is of proper size for their category. You can also assess the coat qualities of the parents. If this is a repeat breeding you may be able to find specimens of the initial breeding to assess for size, coat and type. If this isn't possible, then it might be wise to check animals that have been sired by the father of the puppies you are interested in, or youngsters that have come from the dam by previous matings. By such detective work you will begin to absorb a feeling for the type and kind of animals produced by this particular family and know what to look for in the puppies. Observe particu-

Ch. Alekai Kila, owned by Cesar L. Scaff and Robert M. Krych and bred by Alekai Kennels. Sire: Ch. Ivardon Kenilworth of Ensarr; dam: Ch. Puttencove Kaui. Photo by Ben Burwell.

larly the dam's temperament and her attitude toward her owner. Puppies often copy and mirror their mother's attitudes.

Black is a good color for the novice. Blacks are popular and are generally of good type and sport good coats. Study the pedigree to be sure that the pup has a solid background of black as much as you can determine. Now is the time to try to also find out a bit more than color, size and the show winning propensities of the family. Some strains may be very beautiful and do a great deal of winning, but are basically delicate, poor feeders, uncertain breeders, age early, are prone to illness or are just generally bad doers. Any or all of these hidden factors can be characteristic of a family and it is up to you to find out if they are inherent in the puppies that have caught your interest, for a pup from stock displaying these weaknesses is generally a trial to the novice owner.

Colors in Poodle puppies are often not easy for the neophyte to determine. Puppies can wear a coat color completely different from the color they will sport upon maturity. A black Poodle is born black and a pure white is born white. Brown Poodles are colored a deep brown at birth and gray puppies are born solid black. Whites, creams, and other pale colored puppies are born with pink points (noses, lips, eyerims) which turn to black (or brown) within a few days after birth. All puppies, by the time they are 8 to 10 weeks of age must show the correct points clearly and solidly or they never will. By points I mean, to reiterate, the color of the eyes, nose, lips, eyerims, and claws. All Poodle puppies, with the exception of some apricots, reds, whites and creams, and of course browns, must have dark brown eyes and black points, though in whites the claws are seldom black. The brown Poodle must display brown points. Whites, creams, apricots and reds must have dark eyes and either black or dark brown (liver colored) nose, lips, eye-rims and claws. Black is preferred.

Brown and apricot puppies become paler as they mature, so they must start with dark, rich coloring. Silver puppies, though born black, start turning silver at the feet and around the eyes as they get older. A gray (born black) can be detected within 2 or 3 days after birth by examining the hair between the pads of the feet. If the hair under the feet is gray the puppy will turn gray, if the hair between the pads is black, the pup will be black. It is always difficult, until much later, to determine exactly what shade of gray or silver the animal will exhibit at maturity since gray can range from deep charcoal and blue to a silver approaching white. Generally speaking the hair on the feet between the paws will tell you, most accurately, what color the tiny puppy is destined to be.

Parti-colored Poodles are born either brown and white or black and white. Again examination of the instep hairs gives us the answer to the eventual mature color. If the hairs there are black (assuming the foot itself is colored black), then the Poodle will remain a black and white parti. If the hairs are gray it will become a gray and white parti. Sometimes black and white "phantoms" (partis that display a symmetrical distribution of 2 colors as in the Gordon Setter or the Doberman Pinscher and are emperically black and white or brown and white) are sold as grays. To determine whether they are grays or "phantoms," raise the tail and if you find a triangle of white hair present immediately beneath the tail (and it is there from birth) then the puppy is a "phantom" parti-color, not a gray and not eligible for show ring competition. A Poodle puppy may begin to "clear its color", or begin to exhibit its mature coloring, at from 2 months to a year of age, but not the final adult color shade until it is 18 months old.

Occasionally a puppy's nose will be spotty for a few days or weeks and then turn to its correct color. If you are a purchaser of a pup it is best to take no chances and to select a youngster with a solid colored

Ch. Meisen Bit O' Gold, owned by Hilda Meisenzahl.
Photo by Roberts.

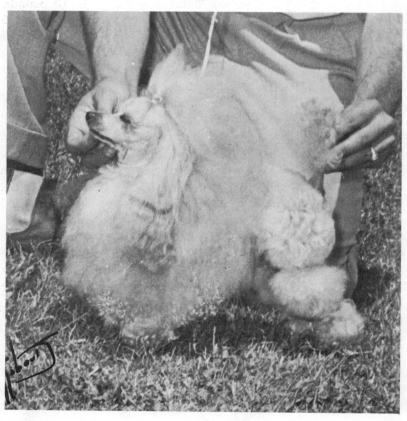

nose. Sometimes adult light apricots and creams develop a paleness of the nose-color, usually during cold weather or after whelping. The eyes will remain dark and so will the other points and the deep color will return again to the nose.

In picking your pup remember that the Standard Poodle is a big dog and should exhibit much bigger bone and less finish than the Miniature of the same age. A Toy will, in turn, be much more balanced and mature appearing than a Miniature of identical age, assuming that they are not very tiny puppies in the nest. The Standard puppy must not only be bigger but must also display the slower development and awkward, "bear-cub" look of a young big animal with the very characteristic bigger and heavier head and ears and floppy-footed rather shambling gait.

A Standard puppy at 8 weeks of age should stand about 9 or 10 inches at the shoulder and weigh approximately 10 pounds. In comparison, a Miniature of the same age will weigh about 3 pounds. If the pups are healthy and have had good care a Standard much under the weight stated, or a Miniature much over, will mature into the medium size so well liked by people who want just a pet but will be useless for show ring competition.

Let me stress again; choose a friendly, gay and active puppy. Look first for a short back that gives the pup a "square" shape. Next look for the long neck and high head carriage that will, upon maturity, lend the dog that elegance that is the Poodle's trademark. See that the tail comes out and up from the top of the back and does not curl. The ears should be low on the head and feel thick to the touch. The eyes should never bulge. They should be dark and almond-shaped, bright and filled with intelligence and mischief. A very slightly Roman-nosed shape to the muzzle is desirable, but it must be slight. The mouth should be level, lips firm, and with the corner, canine teeth, interlocking. Sometimes the baby teeth do not show the correct scissors bite but become normal later when the mature teeth come in. An undershot jaw is a serious fault, so it is best to take no chances and to select a puppy with correct jaws and teeth.

The feet should be small and oval shaped, well knuckled up, and thickly padded. Thin, flat, hare feet should be avoided. Look for straight legs in front, and good angulation with a well-let-down hock in the hindquarters. Examine the hind legs also for a nice flare

Poodles are among the most intelligent of all dog breeds. This great intelligence becomes evident while the puppy is still quite young, and it is at this time that his training should commence for the best possible results. Photo by Louise Van der Meid.

in the stifle, that bend which adds power and curving beauty to the rear assembly.

The coat is very important and also quite difficult to judge in a young puppy since it does not begin to develop into the wanted tight curl until he is about 8 months old. If the coat is thin or spiky (like a Samoyed or Pomeranian) it will never become the type of covering wanted in a Poodle. In a young puppy the coat should be thick and as long as possible. In addition it should appear crimpy and shiny and feel like good Persian lamb to the touch. The coat texture hardens with maturity. If you see that both parents have good coats their puppies will very likely inherit this desirable characteristic.

Watch the way the puppy moves. All puppies are rather clumsy and muscularly soft. If they move out with a trappy, foot-lifting, high-stepping hackney action, the flow of full movement will come with hardening of the muscles, tightening of the tendons, and the control that maturity brings. Remember that the Poodle should move as a hackney horse moves with the power of its hindquarters transmitted through its short, strong back.

Generally the best puppy at eight weeks will be the best one at maturity, too, barring accident or disease. Frequently very fine puppies lose their fine proportions and go awry at from 7 to 9 months of age, a discouraging period for the breeder or owner. It is at this time that many a breeder has sold off a fine puppy and come to regret it. They will come back to their pristine beauty after this period of awkwardness and the ugly duckling again becomes the swan.

Remember, no Poodle ever born has been perfect, but the best have come fairly close to that exalted pinnacle, particularly if they have that extra added bit of elegance, poise, pride and nobility that lifts them above the herd to their own special place in the sun.

By this time you have probably narrowed the field down to one or two puppies. It is time now to hand examine the one or two youngsters who look the best to you. Stand each one upon a table individually in a show stance and examine overall structure. Then examine the mouth for tooth and jaw structure. Next attempt to determine if the pup is sexually whole. At this age the testicles are descended into the scrotum but are often drawn up when the puppy is being handled, making it difficult to locate both testicles during examination. The buyer should have a written agreement with the seller to the effect that, should the puppy prove to be a monorchid or cryptorchid it can be returned and the purchase price refunded or the puppy replaced.

If it is a female puppy you want, look for the same values as outlined above in choosing a male. You would not, of course, go through the performance of determining sex as mentioned above. Female puppies are generally slightly smaller and show a degree of greater refinement than the males.

Remember that no one can pick a champion at eight weeks and no breeder can truthfully sell you a future winner at that age. All a seller can guarantee is the health and breeding of the puppy, and the fact that he possesses the normal complement of eyes, ears and legs. The best you can do if you are observant, knowing and lucky is to pick the best puppy in that particular litter, at that particular time.

If it is at all possible, it is best to purchase two puppies at the same time. They furnish company for each other, eliminate lonesome serenades during the first few nights and are competition at the food pan. If you bring home only one puppy, provide him with a stuffed dog or doll in his sleeping box which you have taken to the sellers with you and rubbed in the nest box. This will frequently give the puppy some sense of comfort and companionship and alleviate the loneliness that brings on dismal howling during the first night in his new home. A ticking alarm clock near the puppy's bed will sometimes have the same effect.

In his new home, amidst strange surroundings, the puppy will very often go off his feed for a time. This should not unduly alarm you unless his refusal to eat lasts so long that he becomes emaciated. If this occurs, ask your veterinarian for a good tonic, or change diets to tempt his palate. Never coax him or resort to forced feeding, or you will immediately spoil your puppy and be a slave to him and his aggravating eating habits from that time forward. If he eats only one or two meals a day, instead of the several feedings he should have, he will survive until his appetite improves if he is otherwise healthy and vigorous. Should you find after a reasonable time and much scheming and effort that you have a naturally finicky eater, you must resign yourself to the fact that you have acquired a headache which can last for the duration of your dog's life and one which cannot be cured by aspirin. Only heroic measures can help you

Encore Silver Showman, owned by Mrs. Jane Fitts.
Photo by Frasie Studio.

conquer this difficulty, and you must steel yourself and cast out pity if you are to succeed. He must be starved, but really starved, until he has reached a point where dry bread resembles the most succulent beef. Only by such drastic measures can a finicky eater be cured. Dogs who have the competition of other dogs, or even a cat, at the feed pan usually display a normal appetite. For this reason it is sometimes smart for the one-dog owner to borrow a friend's or neighbor's pet to feed with his own until such time as his own dog has acquired a healthful and adequate appetite.

Arrange for your puppy to have lots of sleep, particularly after feeding, a difficult chore when there are youngsters in the home, but nevertheless very necessary to the well being of the puppy. Make him feel at home so he will respond quickly to his new surroundings. It so often happens that a puppy retained by the breeder surpasses at maturity the purchased puppy who was a better specimen in the beginning. This confounds the novice, yet has a reasonably simple explanation. The retained pup had no change in environment which would affect his appetite and well being during the critical period of growth, while the bought puppy had and so was outstripped by his lesser litter brother.

Your puppy will have two sets of teeth, the milk teeth, which will have fallen out by the time he is approximately six months of age, and the permanent teeth, which he'll retain for the rest of his life. Loss of weight and fever may accompany the eruption of the new, permanent teeth, but is no cause for alarm. Anatomists have a simple formula to represent the number and arrangement of permanent teeth which, at a glance, will allow you to determine if your dog has his full complement of teeth, and if he hasn't, which ones are missing. In the chart below, the horizontal line represents the division between upper and lower jaw. We begin with the incisors in the front of the dog's mouth and designate them with the letter I. The canine teeth are labeled C, the premolars, P, and the molars, M. The complete formula for a dog possessing all his teeth would be:

$$I\,\frac{3+3}{3+3} + C\,\frac{1+1}{1+1} + P\,\frac{4+4}{4+4} + M\,\frac{2+2}{3+3} = 42\ \text{teeth} \quad \begin{matrix} \text{(20 in upper jaw)} \\ \text{(22 in lower jaw)} \end{matrix}$$

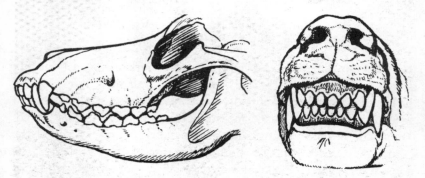

The side and front views of a correct scissors bite. This bite is the most correct for a Poodle and is the most serviceable from a practical point of view.

Occasionally, puppies develop lip warts which will disappear in a short time, leaving no after effects. Remember to have your puppy immunized against distemper and hepatitis and, as much as possible, keep him away from other dogs until he is old enough to combat the diseases which take their toll of the very young. Lastly, but of great importance, give your puppy the opportunity to develop that character and intelligence for which the Poodle is justly famed. Give him human companionship and understanding, take him with you in the car and amongst strangers. Let him live the normal, happy and useful life which is his heritage, and that tiny bundle of wriggles which you brought home so short a time ago will grow into a canine citizen of whom you will be proud to say, "He's mine."

This Poodle prefers Nylabone, a chew toy necessity available at local pet shops (but not in supermarkets). The puppy or grown dog chews the hambone-flavored nylon into a frilly dog toothbrush massaging gums and cleaning his teeth as he plays. Veterinarians highly recommend this product. . . . but beware of cheap imitations that might splinter or break.

Chapter 11
Basic Training for your Poodle

Responsibility for the reputation of any breed is shared by everyone who owns a specimen of that breed. Reputation, good or bad, is achieved by conduct, and conduct is the result of the molding, through training, of inherent character into specific channels of behavior.

It is a distinct pleasure to novice, old-timer or the public at large to watch dogs perform which have been trained to special tasks. Here is the ultimate, the end result of the relationship between man and dog. After watching an inspired demonstration, we sometimes wonder if, under a proper training regime, our own dog could do as well. Perhaps he can if he is temperamentally fitted for the task we have in mind. No single individual of any breed, regardless of breed type, temperament and inheritance, is fitted to cope with all the branches of specialized service. Nor does every owner possess the qualifications or experience necessary to train dogs successfully to arduous tasks. But every dog can be trained in the fundamentals of decent behavior, and every dog owner can give his dog this basic training. It is, indeed, the duty of every dog owner to teach his dog obedience to command as well as the necessary fundamentals of training which insure good conduct and gentlemanly deportment. A dog that is uncontrolled can become a nuisance and even a menace. This dog brings grief to his owner and bad reputation to himself and the breed he represents.

I cannot attempt, in this limited space, to write a complete and comprehensive treatise on all the aspects of dog training. There are several worthwhile books, written by experienced trainers, that cover the entire varied field of initial and advanced training. There are,

No breed of dog adapts more beautifully to training as does a Poodle. This dog, Ch. LaFoy's Little Commotion, C.D., owned by Mr. and Mrs. J. Kilburn King, is a perfect example of what can be accomplished with the breed. This silver Miniature has distinguished himself as a top winner on the bench and in the obedience ring.
Photo by Evelyn Shafer.

furthermore, hundreds of training classes throughout the country where both the dog and its owner receive standard obedience training for a nominal fee, under the guidance of experienced trainers. Here in these pages you will find only specific suggestions on some points of simple basic training which we feel are neglected in most of the books on this subject. We will also attempt to give you basic reasons for training techniques and explain natural limitations to aid you in eliminating future, perhaps drastic, mistakes.

The key to all canine training, simple or advanced, is control. Once you have established control over your Poodle you can, if you so desire, progress to advanced or specialized training. The dog's only boundaries to learning are his own basic limitations. This vital control must be established during the basic training in good manners.

Almost every dog is responsive to training. He loves his master and finds delight in pleasing him. To approach the training problem with your Poodle, to make it a pleasant and easy intimacy rather than an arduous and wearisome task, you must first learn a few fundamentals. In the preceding paragraph I spoke of control as the paramount essential in training. To gain control over your dog, you must first establish control over your own vagaries of temperament. During training, when you lose your temper, you lose control. Shouting, nagging repetition, angry reprimand and exasperation only confuse your canine pupil. If he does not obey, then the lesson has not been learned. He needs teaching, not punishment. The time of training should be approached with pleasure by both master and dog, so that both you and your pupil look forward to these periods of contact. If you establish this atmosphere, your dog will enjoy working, and a dog who enjoys his work, who is constantly trying to please, is a dog who is always under control.

Consistency is the brother of control in training. Perform each movement used in schooling in the same manner every time. Use the same words of command or communication without variance. Employ command words that are simple single syllables, chosen for their crispness and difference in sound. Don't call your dog to you one day with the command "Come," and the next day with the command, "Here," and expect the animal to understand and perform the act with alacrity. Inconsistency confuses your dog. If you are inconsistent, the dog will not perform correctly and your control is lost. By consistency you establish habit patterns which eventually

The first lesson learned by most pet poodles is the proper use of paper. Puppies that have been raised on paper are usually naturally paper trained with no special effort on the part of owner or breeder. Photo by Louise Van der Meid.

become an inherent part of your Poodle's behavior. Remember that a few simple commands, well learned, are much better than many and varied commands only partially absorbed. Therefore be certain that your dog completely understands a command and will perform the action it demands, quickly and without hesitation, before attempting to teach him a new command.

Before we begin training, we must first assess our prospective pupil's intelligence and character. We must understand that his eyesight is not as keen as ours, but that he is quick to notice movement. We must know that sound and scent are his chief means of communication with his world, and that in these departments he is far superior to us. We must reach him, then, through voice and gesture, and realize that he is very sensitive to quality, change and intonation of the commanding voice. Therefore, any given command must have a definite tonal value in keeping with its purpose. The word "no" used in reprimand must be expressed sharply and with overtones of displeasure, while "good boy," employed as praise, should be spoken lightly and pleasantly. In early training, the puppy

Dorleen's Mystic Moselle, U.D., owned by Eileen P. Larkin.
Photo by Evelyn Shafer.

It is natural for a Poodle to jump on a person in the manner of greeting. This can be a problem, especially with a Standard. This tendency can be discouraged by bumping the dog lightly with the knee in his chest each time he jumps up. Photo by Louise Van der Meid.

recognizes distinctive sound coupled with the quality of tone used rather than individual words.

All words of positive command should be spoken sharply and distinctly during training. By this we do not mean that commands must be shouted, a practice which seems to be gaining favor in obedience work and which is very much to be deplored. A well-trained mature Poodle can be kept completely under control and will obey quickly and willingly when commands are given in an ordinary conversational tone. The first word a puppy learns is the word-sound of his name; therefore, in training, his name should be spoken first to attract his attention to the command which follows. Thus, when we want our dog to come to us, and his name is Brandy, we command, "Brandy! Come!"

Intelligence varies in dogs as it does in all animals, human or otherwise. The ability to learn and to perform is limited by intelligence, facets of character and structure, such as willingness, energy, sensitivity, aggressiveness, stability and functional ability. The sensitive dog must be handled with greater care and quietness in training than the less sensitive animal. Aggressive dogs must be trained with firmness, and an animal which possesses a structural fault which makes certain of the physical aspects of training a painful experience cannot be expected to perform these acts with enjoyment and consistency.

In referring to intelligence, we mean, of course, canine intelligence. Dogs are supposedly unable to reason, since that portion of the brain which, in humans, is the seat of the reasoning power is not highly developed in the dog. Yet there have been so many reported incidents of canine behavior that seemingly could not have been actuated by instinct, training, stored knowledge or the survival factor that we are led to wonder if the dog may not possess some primitive capacity for reasoning which, in essence, is so different from the process of human reasoning that it has been overlooked, or is as yet beyond the scope of human comprehension.

Training begins the instant the puppies in the nest feel the touch of your hand and are able to hear the sound of your voice. Once the pup is old enough to run and play, handle him frequently, petting him, making a fuss over him, speaking in soothing and pleasant tones and repeating his name over and over again. When you bring him his meals, call him by name and coax him to "come." As time

A dog that is trained to heel on leash is always a better companion and a greater source of pleasure than one that pulls and strains, hangs back or runs wildly in any direction he pleases. Photo by Louise Van der Meid.

passes, he associates the command "come" with a pleasurable experience and will come immediately upon command. Every time he obeys a command, he should be praised or rewarded. When calling your puppies to their food, it is good practice to use some kind of distinguishing sound accompanying the command—a clucking or "beep" sound. It is amazing how this distinctive sound will be retained by the dog's memory, so that years after it has ceased to be used, he will still remember and respond to the sound.

Some professional trainers and handlers put soft collars on tiny pups, with a few inches of thin rope attached to the collar clip. The puppies, in play, tug upon these dangling pieces of rope hanging from the collars of their litter mates, thus preparing the youngsters for easy leash breaking in the future. In training the pup to the leash, be sure to use a long leash, and coax, do not drag, the reluctant puppy,

Getting a young dog used to the leash should be done in a gentle, gradual manner. It is of vital importance that the dog be properly leash trained in the light of the many dangers that exist today from automobiles and dog thieves. Photo by Louise Van der Meid.

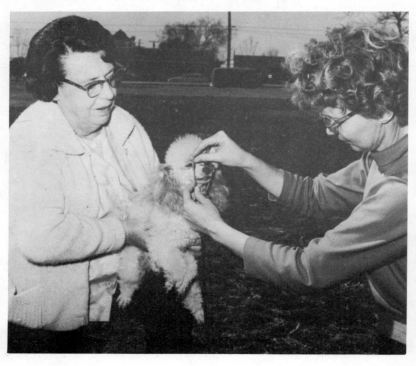

Charbon Camee of Puttencove, C.D.X., owned by Betty Van Sciver and Ma Folie Meredith, C.D.X., owned by Mrs. Carl Necker execute a variation on the standard high jump. There have been many instances of Poodles like these trained for special exhibitions and trick work. Photo by Evelyn Shafer.

keeping him always on your left side. Never use the leash as an implement of punishment.

Housebreaking is usually the tragedy of the novice dog owner. Many Poodles which are raised outside in a run never need to be actually housebroken, preferring to use the ground for their act and seemingly sensing the fact that the house is not to be soiled. Dogs tend to defecate in areas which they, or other dogs, have previously soiled, and will go to these spots if given the chance. Directly after eating or waking a puppy almost inevitably has to relieve himself. If he is in the house and makes a mistake, it is generally your fault, as you should have recognized these facts and removed him in time to avert disaster. If, after you have taken him out, he comes in and soils the floor or rug, he must be made to realize that he has done wrong. Scold him with "Shame! Shame!" and rush him outside. Praise him extravagantly when he has taken advantage of the great outdoors. Sometimes if you catch him preparing to void in the house, a quick, sharp "No" will stop the proceedings and allow you time to usher him out. Never rub his nose in his excreta. Never indulge in the common practice of striking the puppy with a rolled up newspaper or with your hand. If you do, you may be training your dog either to be hand shy, be shy of paper, or to bite the newsboy. Your hand should be used only in such a way that your dog recognizes it as that part of you which implements your voice, to pet and give pleasure. In housebreaking, a "No" or "Shame" appropriately used and delivered in an admonishing tone is punishment enough.

Scent discrimination, one of the most difficult and demanding of the obedience exercises requires that the dog choose an article from among a number of articles. The judge or steward will plant them while the dog and handler are looking away after which the dog must complete the exercise successfully. Photo by Louise Van der Meid.

Retrieving is instinctive to a Poodle regardless of his size. The breed has proven its ability in this and other obedience areas time after time, and the Poodle is one of the most frequently seen breeds in obedience trials. Photo by Louise Van der Meid.

A dog which will attain the size of a Standard Poodle is seldom broken to paper in the house. If your dog has been so trained and subsequently you wish to train him to use the outdoors, a simple way to teach him this is to move the paper he has used outside, anchoring it with stones. Lead the dog to the paper when you know he is ready to void. Each day make the paper smaller until it has completely disappeared, and the pup will have formed the habit of going on the spot previously occupied by the paper. Puppies tend to prefer to void on a surface similar in texture to that which they used in their first few weeks of life. Thus a puppy who has had access to an outside run is easily housebroken, preferring the feel of ground under him. Miniatures and Toys are sometimes raised on wire-bottom pens to keep them free of intestinal parasites. Occasionally puppies so raised have been brought into homes with central heating employing an

Most Poodles love to jump, but sometimes one will be reluctant to undergo exercises in directed jumping. The owner should stand off a bit and encourage the dog to take the jump. Photo by Louise Van der Meid.

With directed jumping it often helps at the outset of training, to take the jump alongside the dog. When the dog gets the idea and has gained a bit of confidence in himself, he will eagerly take the jump without assistance. Photo by Louise Van der Meid.

open grate-covered duct in the floor. To the pup the grate feels similar to his former wire-bottomed pen. The result, as you can well imagine, gives rise to much profanity and such diligence that the youngster is either rapidly housebroken or just as rapidly banished to live outdoors.

If your Poodle is to be a housedog, a lot of grief can be avoided by remembering a few simple rules. Until he is thoroughly clean in the house, confine him to one room at night, preferably a tile-or linoleum-floored room that can be cleaned easily. Tie him so that he cannot get beyond the radius of his bed, or confine him to a dog house within the room; few dogs will soil their beds or sleeping quarters. Feed at regular hours and you will soon learn the interval

In retrieving exercises, the dog is expected to sit squarely in front of the handler, holding the dumbell in his mouth until the handler takes it, at which time the dog should give it up without any kind of struggle. Photo by Louise Van der Meid.

between the meal and its natural result and take the puppy out in time. Give water only after meals until he is housebroken. Puppies, like inveterate drunks, will drink constantly if the means is available, and there is no other place for surplus water to go but out. The result is odd puddles at odd times.

"No," "Shame," "Come," and "Good boy" (or "girl"), spoken in appropriate tones, are the basic communications you will use in initial training.

If your pup is running free and he doesn't heed your command to come, do not chase him—he will only run away or dodge your attempts to catch him and your control over him will be completely lost. Attract his attention by calling his name and, when he looks in your direction, turn and run away from him, calling him as you do so.

This Miniature has chosen a glove from scent discrimination articles and is returning it to his handler. A dog can also be just as easily trained to carry a newspaper or a small bag of groceries. Photo by Louise Van der Meid.

In most instances he will quickly run after you. Even if it takes a great deal of time and much exasperation to get him to come to you, never scold him once he has. Praise him instead. *A puppy should only be scolded when he is caught in the act of doing something he shouldn't do.* If he is scolded even a few minutes after he has committed his error, he will not associate the punishment with the crime and will be bewildered and unhappy about the whole thing, losing his trust in you.

Puppies are inveterate thieves. It is natural for them to steal food from the table. The "No!" and "Shame!" command, or reprimand, should be used to correct this breach of manners. The same commands are employed when the pup uses your living room couch as a

Competitors in advanced obedience usually have a small bag or box, such as the one pictured, in which to store and carry dumbells and other obedience articles for the various tests and exercises their dogs must undergo. Photo by Louise Van der Meid.

A dog is taught to "stand-stay" by the command "stay" and the hand put in front of the dog's face as shown. This command renders a dog under far greater control at all times. Photo by Louise Van der Meid.

sleeping place. Many times dogs are aware that they must not sleep on the furniture, but are clever enough to avoid punishment by using the sofa only when you are out. They will hastily leave the soft comfort of the couch when they hear you approaching and greet you in wide-eyed innocence, models of canine virtue. Only the tell-tale hairs, the dent in the cushion, and the body heat on the fabric are clues to the culprit's dishonesty. This recalls the tale of the dog who went just a step further. So clever was he that when his master approached, he would leap from the couch and, standing before it, blow upon the cushions to dislodge the loose hairs and cool the cushion's surface. The hero of this tale of canine duplicity was not identified as to breed, but I am sure that such intelligence could only have been displayed by a Poodle.

If, like the dog in the story, the puppy persists in committing this misdemeanor, we must resort to another method to cure him. Where before we used a positive approach, we must now employ a negative, and rather sneaky, method. The idea is to trick the pup into thinking that when he commits these crimes he punishes himself and that we have been attempting to stop him from bringing this punishment down upon his head. To accomplish this end with the unregenerate food thief, tie a tempting morsel of food to a long piece of string. To the string attach several empty tin cans, or small bells, eight to ten inches apart. Set the whole contraption on the kitchen or dining-room table, with the food morsel perched temptingly on an accessible edge. Leave the room and allow the little thief to commit his act of dishonesty. When you hear the resultant racket, rush into the room, sternly mouthing the appropriate words of reproach. You will generally find a thoroughly chastened pup who, after one or two such lessons, will eye any tabled food askance and leave it strictly alone.

The use of mousetraps is a neat little trick to cure the persistent sofa-hopper. Place two or three set traps on the couch area the dog prefers and cover them with a sheet of newspaper. When he jumps up on the sofa, he will spring the traps and leave that vicinity in a great and startled hurry.

These methods, or slight variations, can be used in teaching your pup to resist many youthful temptations such as dragging and biting rugs, furniture, tablecloths, draperies, curtains, etc.

The same approach, in essence, is useful in teaching the pup not to

A Poodle is a real fun dog. He takes readily to training, and is a gentle pet and companion. Your Poodle craves love and human companionship. This love in combination with proper training makes the Poodle an unbeatable pet. Photo by Louise Van der Meid.

jump up on you or your friends and neighbors. You can lose innumerable friends if your mud-footed dog playfully jumps up on the visitor wearing a new suit or dress. If the "No" command alone does not break him of this habit, hold his front legs and feet tightly in your hands when he jumps up, and retain your hold. The pup finds himself in an uncomfortable and unnatural position standing on his hind legs alone. He will soon tug and pull to release his front legs from your hold. Retain your hold in the face of his struggles until he is heartily sick of the strained position he is in. A few such lessons and he will refrain from committing an act which brings such discomfort in its wake.

Remember that only by positive training methods can you gain control which is the basis of successful training, and these tricky methods do not give you that control. They are simply short-cut ways of quickly rectifying nuisance habits, but do nothing to establish the "rapport" which must exist between trainer and dog.

During the entire puppy period the basis is being laid for other and more advanced training. The acts of discipline, of everyday handling, grooming and feeding, are preparation for the time when he is old enough to be taught the meaning of the Sit, Down, Heel, Stand, and Stay, commands, which are the first steps in obedience training and commands which every dog should be taught to obey immediately. Once you have learned how to train your dog and have established complete control, further training is only limited by your own abilities and by the natural boundaries which exist within the animal himself.

Don't rush your training. Be patient with small progress. Training for both you and your dog will become easier as you progress. Make sure that whatever you teach him is well and thoroughly learned, and it will never be forgotten.

Chapter 12
Training the Poodle for the Show Ring

So many things of beauty or near perfection are so often marred and flawed by an improper approach to their finish. A Renoir or an El Greco tacked frameless to a bathroom wall is no less a thing of art, yet loses importance by its limited environment and presentation. Living things, too, need this finish and preparation to exhibit their worth to full advantage. The beauty of a flower goes unrecognized if withered petals and leaves mar its perfection, and the living wonder of a fine dog is realized only in those moments when he stands or moves in quiet and balanced beauty. The show ring is a ready frame in which to display your dog. The manner in which he is presented within the frame is up to you.

If you contemplate showing your Poodle as so many of you who read this book do, it is of the utmost importance that your dog be as well and fully trained for exhibition as he is for general gentlemanly conduct in the home, Insufficient or improper training, or faulty handling, can result in lower show placings than your dog deserves and can quite conceivably ruin an otherwise promising show career. In the wider sense, and of even more importance to the breed as a whole, is the impression your Poodle in the show ring projects to the gallery. Every Poodle shown becomes a representative of the breed in the eyes of the onlookers, so that each dog becomes a symbol of all Poodles when he is on exhibition. Inside the ring ropes, your dog will be evaluated by the judges as an individual; beyond the ropes, a breed will be judged by the behavior of your dog. So often the abominable behavior of an untrained animal irks even those whose interest lies with the breed. Think, then, what a warped impression of the breed must be conveyed, by this same animal, to the critically watching ringsider.

When you enter your Poodle in a show, you do so because you believe that he or she is a good enough specimen of the breed to afford competition to, and perhaps win over, the other dogs entered. If your Poodle is as good as you think he is, he certainly deserves to be shown to full advantage if you expect him to win a place in this highly competitive sport. A novice handler with a quality Poodle which is untrained, unruly or phlegmatic cannot give competition to a dog of equal, or even lesser merit which is well trained and handled to full advantage.

Novice owners frequently bring untrained dogs to shows so that they can become accustomed to the strange proceedings and sur-

Patient, consistent training is needed for the show Poodle. He will accept show handling if he is started at an early age. In this way, he will be a joy to handle when he is ready to do some serious winning. Photo by Louise Van der Meid.

Miniature and Toy puppies should become accustomed to being handled on a table or other raised surface. With the smaller varieties judges often do their examinations on a table and a dog who has not been trained to expect this in the ring will not make the best of itself under such circumstances. Photo by Louise Van der Meid.

roundings, hopefully thinking that, in time, the dog will learn to behave in the wanted manner by himself. Often the novice's training for the show ring begins in desperate and intense endeavor within the show ring itself. Confusion for both dog and handler can be the only result of such a program. Preparation for showing must begin long in advance of actual show competition for both dog and handler.

Let us assume that you have been fortunate enough to breed or purchase a puppy who appears to possess all the necessary qualifications for a successful show career. Training for that career should begin from the moment you bring him home, or if you are the breeder, from the time he is weaned. This early training essentially follows the same pattern as does fundamental training in conduct. Again you begin by establishing between you and the puppy the happy relationship which, in time, becomes the control so necessary to all training. Handle the puppy frequently, brush him, examine his

Many Poodle exhibitors keep their dogs in wire crates while they are on the showbench. This is designed for the comfort of the dogs, so that they will not be fed or handled by spectators in the course of a show and so that they can get some much needed rest when they are not being groomed or in the ring being shown.

The best way to set up a Poodle's front is, by holding him behind the shoulders, lifting him a few inches off the ground and letting him come down slowly and carefully. Photo by Louise Van der Meid.

teeth, set him up in a show stance, and stroke his back slowly. Move him on a loose leash, talking to him constantly in a happy, friendly tone. Make all your movements in a deliberate and quiet manner. Praise and pat the puppy often, establishing an easy and happy rapport during this period. This is simple early preparation for the more exact training to come.

During this period the owner and prospective handler should take the opportunity to refresh or broaden his own knowledge. Reread the standard, and with this word picture in mind, build a mental reproduction of the perfect Poodle: his structure, balance and gait. Critically observe the better handlers at shows to see how they set and gait their dogs. Only by accumulating insight and knowledge such as this can you succeed in the training which will bring out the best features of your own future show dog.

Let us assume that your puppy is now old enough to show, or that you have acquired a young dog for whom you plan a show career. Beginning long before the show in which you are going to start him (several weeks at least), you introduce him to the "tidbit." This can be any bit of food which the dog relishes immensely and which is entirely different from the kind of food used in his regular diet. The tidbit, then, is a tasty piece of food which the dog likes and which is not given to him at any other time. Boiled liver, in chunks, is most generally used, but dogs can be shown with liverwurst, peanuts, turkey or various other treats which the individual animal might particularly relish. If you choose liver as your tidbit, brown it in the oven for a few minutes after you have boiled it. This tends to remove the greasiness from the surface and keeps it from crumbling excessively, making it much easier to handle and carry in your pocket in the show ring. Also, available at practically every pet retail counter are ready-made treats produced for training and show purposes. These treats or tidbits are very effective and inexpensive, and further relegate the burden of production into the hands of the manufacturer.

To set your puppy up in the correct show ring stance, pull the collar loop high to where the neck joins the head and so that the ends of the collar, which should be slightly slack, are directly behind the ears. Holding the lead taut above the dog to keep its head high, see that the front legs form a straight vertical line, feet pointing directly forward and elbows flat against the body. This can sometimes be accomplished by lifting the dog up while holding the sides of his head from in front and dropping his feet gently down again to the ground.

When you have head, neck and front as they should be, switch your lead to the right hand and lift the rear end of your dog up gently by the crotch and lower him. Make sure that the hind legs are not too closely set. The hocks should form a 95 degree angle with the floor. The back should be straight, with no middle sag. Both front and hind legs can also be set separately by hand without lifting, if the dog falls into a good stance naturally. Now show your Poodle the tidbit. Make him stand without moving by the "stay" command, his eyes and sharp attention on the tidbit. Give him an occasional tiny taste to keep his continued interest.

The Poodle is supposed to be shown on a loose leash, both standing and moving. The leash should be switched again to the left hand after the dog has been set up, though some handlers retain the leash in the right hand so that the left hand is free to hold up the tail.

When moving the Poodle the leash is held in the left hand, the head kept high and the dog moved forward in a collected, easy trot. Use the tidbit as bait, tempting the Poodle with it as you move him. This will keep his head up and gain his eager attention. When you come to the end of the allotted run and turn to start back, do not jerk the dog around; instead allow him to come around easily without a change of leads, meanwhile speaking to him quietly. When he has completed the turn continue moving back to the starting point. At the finish, pat and praise him.

While you are teaching your dog the elements of ring deportment, take stock of the pupil himself. To do this correctly, you will need assistance. Have someone else put the dog through his paces, handling him as you have and as he will be handled in the show ring. Observe the dog carefully to determine when he looks his best. Should he be stretched out a bit when posing? Or does he have better balance and outline if his hind legs are not pulled too far back? At what rate of speed, when moving, does he perform his best?

Pretend that you are a judge. Envision the perfect Poodle, and employing your knowledge of the standard as a yardstick, study your dog as though he were a strange animal. From this study you will see many things, tiny nuances, that will aid you in showing your Poodle to the best possible advantage in open competition.

Once he has mastered the show training you have given him, you must take every opportunity to allow strangers and friends to go over your dog, much in the manner of a judge, while you pose and gait him, so he will become used to a judge's unaccustomed liberties. It would be well to enter your Poodle in a few outdoor sanction matches now, to acquaint him with the actual conditions under which he will be shown. During all this time, of course, the character and temperament of your dog, as well as his physical assets, must be taken into consideration, as it must in all types of training, and the most made of the best he has.

Often a handler showing a dog which has not had sufficient training must use other methods to get the most from the animal. We must remember, too, that unless specifically trained to one particular method, a dog may be presented to better advantage when handled in an entirely different manner. It is necessary to attract the attention of some dogs by strange noises, either oral or mechani-

Ch. Wilber White Swan, owned by Bertha Smith. This white Toy was best in show at the Westminster Kennel Club in 1956. This event marked the first time in the history of this great dog club that a toy breed carried off the top prize. The judge here was Paul Palmer and the handler was Anne Rogers Clark. Club President William A. Rockefeller appears center. Photo by Evelyn Shafer.

Ch. Puttencove Promise, owned by Puttencove Kennels. A white Standard, this dog was best in show at the Westminster Kennel Club in 1958 under judge W. W. Brainard, Jr. He was the second of his variety to take best in show here and the first Standard to do so since 1935. He was shown by the late Robert Gorman. Club President William A. Rockefeller is at the right. Photo by Evelyn Shafer.

Ch. Fontclair Festoon, owned by Dunwalke Kennels. This English Imported black Miniature bitch was best in show at the Westminster Kennel Club in 1959. She was the second of her variety to go best in show here and the first since 1943. She was handled by Anne Rogers Clark. Photo by Evelyn Shafer.

cal. You will also often see handlers squat down on the right side of their animals and set the dogs' legs and feet in the desired position. But dogs set up by hand in this manner generally lack the grace and flow of lines that the naturally posed dog shows to such good advantage.

There is, of course, that paragon of all show dogs, that canine jewel and handler's delight—the alert, curious animal who takes a keen interest in the world around him, posing every minute he is in the ring. But remember, even this super-show dog has had some training in ring manners.

In some instances the dog's master stands outside of the ring in full view of his animal while someone else handles him in the ring. The dog will watch his master, keeping his head up and wearing an alert expression. This is called "double-handling," and is frowned upon by other members of the showing fraternity.

It is of the utmost importance that you never become blind to your dog's faults, but at the same time realize his good features and attempt to exploit these when in the ring. If your dog is a year old, or older, do not feed him the day before the show. This will make him more eager for the tidbit when in the ring. Make sure your dog is in good physical shape, in good coat, clean and well groomed. Be sure he is not thirsty when he enters the ring and that he has emptied himself before showing, or it will cramp his movement and make him uncomfortable.

School yourself to be at ease in the ring when handling your dog, for if you are tense and nervous, it will communicate itself to the dog, and he will display the same emotional stress. In the ring, keep one eye on your dog and the other on the judge. One never knows when a judge might turn from the animal he is examining, look at your dog, and perhaps catch him in an awkward moment.

Before showing trim any ragged hair to leave a trim, sculptured outline. If his claws need clipping, tend to it at least four days before show time so that if you should cut too deeply, the claw will have time to heal.

On the morning of the show, leave your home early enough so that you will have plenty of time to be benched and tend to any last minute details which may come up. When the class before yours is in the ring, give your dog a last quick brush.

Bring to the show with you: a water pail, towel, brush, comb, suppositories in a small jar, a bench chain, scissors, and a light slip leash for showing. If the dog has not emptied himself, insert a suppository in his rectum when you take him to the exercising ring. If you forget to bring the suppositories, use instead two paper matches, wet with saliva, from which you have removed the sulphur tips.

Following is a chart listing the dog-show classes and indicating elibigility in each class, with appropriate remarks. This chart will tell you at a glance which is the best class for your dog.

DOG-SHOW CLASS CHART

Class	Eligible Dogs	Remarks
PUPPY—6 months and under 9 months	All puppies from 6 months up to 9 months.	Can be shown in puppy clip. Canadian and American bred only.
PUPPY—9 months and under 12 months	All puppies from 9 months to 12 months.	After 12 months must be shown in adult show clip.
NOVICE	Any dog or puppy which has not won an adult class (over 12 months), or any higher award, at a point show.	After 3 first-place Novice wins, cannot be shown again in the class.
BRED BY EXHIBITOR	Any dog or puppy, other than a Champion, which is owned and bred by exhibitor.	Must be shown only by a member of immediate family of breeder-exhibitor, *i.e.*, husband, wife, father, mother, son, daughter, brother, sister.
AMERICAN-BRED	All dogs or puppies whelped in the U.S. or possessions, except Champions.	
OPEN DOGS	All dogs, 6 months of age or over, including Champions and foreign-breds.	Canadian and foreign champions are shown in open until acquisition of American title. By common courtesy, most American Champions are entered only in Specials.
SPECIALS CLASS	American Champions.	Compete for B.O.V., for which no points are given.

The properly trained show Poodle should present a picture of un-
matched canine elegance. It is only through proper training that the
Poodle will learn to put his best foot forward and always make the
most of himself in the ring. Photo by Louise Van der Meid.

Each sex is judged separately. The winners of each class compete against each other for Winners and Reserve Winners. The animal designated as Winner is awarded the points. Reserve Winners receives no points. Reserve Winners can be the second dog in the class from which the Winners Dog was chosen. The Winners Male and Winners Female (Winners Dog and Winners Bitch) compete for Best of Winners. The one chosen Best of Winners competes against the Specials for Best of Variety, and the Best of Variety winner goes into the Variety Group. If fortunate enough to top this group, the final step is to compete against the other group winners for the Best in Show title.

When the Best of Variety is awarded, Best of Opposite Sex is also chosen. A Poodle which has taken the points in its own sex as Winners, yet has been defeated for Best of Winners, can still be awarded Best of Opposite Sex if there are no animals of its sex appearing in the ring for the Best of Variety award.

Champions are made by the point system. Only the Winners Dog and Winners Bitch receive points, and the amount of points won depends upon the number of Poodles of its own sex the dog has defeated in the classes (not by the number entered) and in its variety. The United States is divided into five regional point groups by the A.K.C., and the point rating varies with the region in which the show is held. Consult a show catalogue for regional rating. A Poodle going Best of Winners is allowed the same number of points as the animal of the opposite sex which it defeats if the points are of a greater amount than it won by defeating members of its own sex. No points are awarded for Best of Variety.

To become a Champion, a dog must win fifteen points under a minimum of three different judges. In accumulating these points, the dog must win points in at least two major (three points or more) shows, under different judges. Five points is the maximum amount that can be won at any given show. If your Poodle wins a group, he is entitled to the highest number of points won in any of the breeds by the dogs he defeats in the group if the points exceed the amount he has won in his own breed. If the show is a Poodle Specialty, then the Best of Breed winner automatically becomes the Best in Show dog. No points are awarded at Match or Sanctioned shows.

Remember that showing is a sport, not a matter of life and death, so take your lickings with the same smile that you take your winnings, even if it hurts (and it does). Tomorrow is another day, another show, another judge. The path of the show dog is never strewn with roses, though it may look that way to the novice handler who seems, inevitably, to step on thorns. Always be a good sport, don't run the other fellow's dog down because he has beaten yours, and when a Poodle goes into the group, give him your hearty applause even if you don't like the dog, his handler, his owner, and his breeding, Remember only that he is a Poodle, a representative of your breed and therefore the finest dog in the group.

We hope that this chapter will help the novice show handler to find greater ease and surety in training for show and handling in the ring and thus experience more pleasure from exhibiting. Competition is the spice of life, and a good Poodle should be shown to its best advantage, for its own glory and for the greater benefit of a wonderful breed.

Chapter 13

How to Clip your Poodle

To keep your Poodle attractive and clean takes constant grooming and frequent clipping and trimming. The cost of such attention can be considerable when the owner must depend upon canine beauty parlors for this service.

As a result, many people who are attracted to the breed feel that they cannot afford the expense involved in frequent and periodic clipping by professionals and, unless they are more financially solvent than most of us in this era of soaring living costs and high taxes, they are certainly correct in this assumption. The costs involved should make the Poodle an allowable tax exemption as a dependent though the Federal Government would take a dim view of this arrangement. But, in a more serious vein, these cosmetic costs can build a monetary barrier to the continued popularity of a wonderful breed.

Unfortunately, due to the fine quality and profuseness of the Poodle's coat, lack of frequent barbering quickly results in an odorous mess that makes the animal uncomfortable and objectionable both to itself and to those who live with it.

CLIPPING EQUIPMENT

Clipping your Poodle takes time, skill, and a period of learning. But, if you have the proper tools, the knowledge, a little patience, and if you can use your hands, you can acquire the skill and learn to clip your Poodle as well as any professional and derive pleasure and save money in the process.

You will acquire the necessary knowledge of the clipping procedure in these pages. You will also find out what clipping equipment you should use and how to use it. The extent of your patience, the dexterity of your hands, and your mental ability are for you to decide.

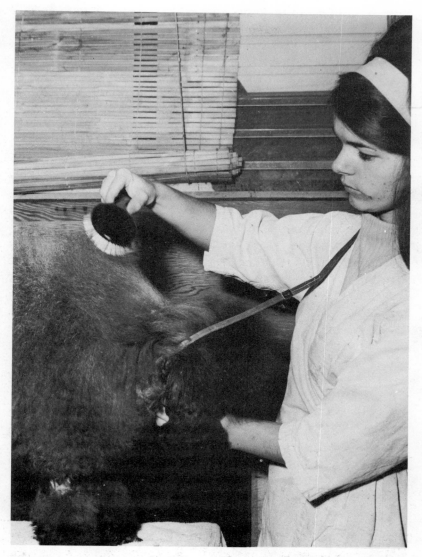

Clipping a Poodle is as much a matter of conditioning as much as cutting. This is especially true of show clips where the coat must be regularly worked over a long period of time to bring it into peak condition. Photo by Louise Van der Meid.

The truth is that many professional groomers, so as not to lose your business, attempt to make you appear an idiot if they surmise that you intend to learn how to clip your own dog. It is not the frightening chore they make it appear to be. At first it may not be easy, but then, nothing that is worthwhile doing is easy at the beginning.

Now, let us proceed to the tools you will need to work with. Select a table (a card table is a good height), box or crate on which to place your dog while you clip him. Be sure that the height of this platform will allow you to work with comfort and ease without undue bending. An arm, of metal preferably, or of wood, in the form of a reversed L should be fastened firmly to the clipping platform, the horizontal arm high enough to allow about a foot of space above the head of your Poodle when it stands on the platform. A light leash or chain attached to this overhead arm and fastened to the collar of your dog will help to hold and steady him leaving your hands free to

A table of convenient height, placed in a well-lighted area is practically a necessity for any Poodle grooming. Many people are not aware of how much more well-behaved a dog is on the table and how much easier this makes any attempt at grooming or trimming. Photo by Louise Van der Meid.

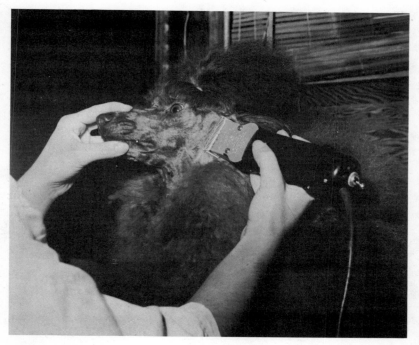

Any one who plans to groom Poodles must have a small electric animal clipper such as the one shown. It is a good idea to have several different sized blades in order to clip hair of various required lengths. Photo by Louise Van der Meid.

perform their task. This "L" or "grooming stand" can be ordered from your petshop.

The most important item of necessary equipment is, of course, the electric small animal hair clipper. There are several brands and prices can range from ten dollars to fifty dollars according to quality. There is even a set being marketed for human barbering containing a plastic clipper, shears, comb, etc., that is priced at under ten dollars and will do a good job of clipping for the novice who simply wants to keep his pet well groomed. Cheaper clippers will probably give less service than expensive ones, within reason. But, remember that unless you keep a kennel of Poodles, an inexpensive clipper that works well will give your adequate service since you will not be using it too frequently. Kennel owners and professionals must necessarily have the best for nothing less would stand up under the constant use.

The electric clipper will always cut closer if it is run against the lay of the hair. This allows the operator to pick up hair ends missed on the first pass without the need to change blades. Photo by Louise Van der Meid.

You should, though, purchase a clipper with interchangeable heads so that you can, when you become expert, use blades of different sizes.

Lower blade, numbers will be the most useful to the average Poodle owner. The medium blade is recommended for general usage for the novice who is just learning to clip. It is less likely to irritate or nick the skin of your Poodle.

The higher the number the closer the blade will clip. A coarser cutting blade is often recommended for the Dutch and Retriever clips, especially for Toys. A very fine blade will cut too close and should only be used (and then very carefully) by professionals. Remember that ANY blade will cut closer AGAINST the grain, or lay of coat, than it will when applied WITH the lay of coat. The finer the blade the closer the clip. A fine blade will cut the hair to within 1/32" of the skin. A skip-tooth blade allows long, shaggy coats to be fed with greater rapidity to the cutting edge and is particularly useful when clipping Standard Poodles.

Keep your clippers cleaned and oiled and, when you have completed the clipping job, sweep up and remove all loose hair from the vicinity in which you have been working so that your clipping corner is clean and ready for the next session.

A steel comb and a pair of barber's shears are the next items in importance. Following these you will want a stiff brush and a grooming glove (see "Grooming" section in chapter on general care).

Barber's shears are useful for finishing. With your shears you can snip away stray ends of hair and shape the pompoms and all-over outline much as a gardener trims a hedge.

A plucking or razor-blade dresser will also aid in the end result by giving your Poodle's clip a finished and professional appearance.

Part of the regular grooming routine for all Poodles should be a check on the ears and the removal of excess hair and wax if any is present. The operator is using a surgical hemostat to clean the hair out of this Poodle's ears. Photo by Louise Van der Meid.

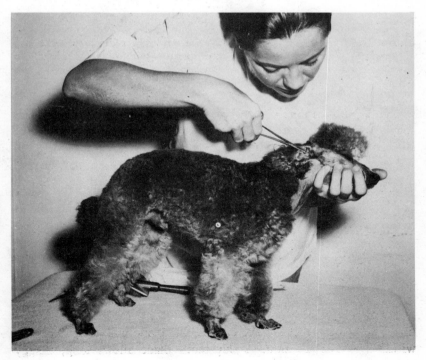

The razor-blade dresser is used to smooth away coat cut marks and any small unevenness where the coat is clipped too closely.

The owner of a pet Poodle who has no show ring ambitions and who merely wishes to keep his pet looking neat and well-groomed, actually needs only the electric clipper, brush, claw clippers, comb and shears. Those who wish to show their animals will gradually develop the necessary skill in barbering through practice and will then want other tools to add a professional touch to the finished product.

HOW TO CLIP YOUR POODLE

If your dog has never before been clipped, the sound of the running clipper may disturb him. To keep him from forming a habit-pattern of nervousness and fear that will manifest itself each time you attempt to clip him, the approach this initial time must be made with caution. Put your Poodle on the clipping table and show him the clipper and allow him to sniff it. Then turn the clipper

Extremely gentle handling is vital when using clippers on a puppy for the first time. If a puppy is made to understand that he will not be hurt by trimming, he will always be an easy subject to work on. Photo by Louise Van der Meid.

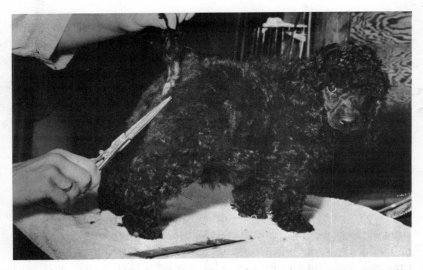

A Poodle puppy must learn to be still and composed during trimming sessions. A dog's safety during trimming often depends on his deportment. An unruly animal is much more prone to injury by the scissor than is a dog that can be expected to act right. Photo by Louise Van der Meid.

on and hold it in your hand while you talk to him in a light, friendly tone, assuring him that there is nothing to fear from the buzz. Next turn the clipper off and run it through his coat and around his head a few times until he has lost all fear of it. You can then begin the actual operation of clipping him quietly and gently talking as you cut to calm his natural fears.

Hold the flat of the clipper blade against the surface you are clipping. If you tip it forward it will dig in and cause unsightly cut marks. Remember not to cut against the grain or lay of the hair, always clip with the grain. Later, when you have become expert, there may be some areas (around the lips, throat, etc.) where you will perhaps want to cut closer and, with the skill you have acquired, it will be possible for you to clip against the lay of the hair. Actually, only a show Poodle need ever be trimmed this closely. The ordinary house pet doesn't need as fine a finish as the show Poodle. Cutting against the grain can cause sharp and uneven crevices in the clipped area and burn the dog's tender skin causing scabs to form. The burning of clipper cutting against the grain can build an avid dislike for the whole business in the mind of your Poodle, and he will forever after be difficult to manage during the clipping process. Start clipping your Poodle when he is young, anytime after three months of age. Begin by clipping the feet, base of tail and foreface. If he raises an objection when you know you are not hurting him, be firm, insist that he stand for his barbering and, after a time or two, he will become accustomed to the process and will either be eager for the attention clipping brings or bored with the whole thing.

The first time you clip your Poodle be content with simply using the clippers, particularly if it is also the first time for your dog. Once both you and the dog gain confidence you can graduate to the use of the other tools. When using the shears always have the points angled away from the dog's eyes for a quick move by the dog can be disastrous if they are pointed toward the eyes.

Incidentally, many Poodles are taught to lie quietly on their backs and sides for the clipping of specific sections of the body. Powder, applied immediately to the part just clipped is also used.

In a pet clip, if the Poodle is to wear face furnishings, those furnishings should be trimmed to neatness and any discolored hairs which may be present should be removed. Photo by Louise Van der Meid.

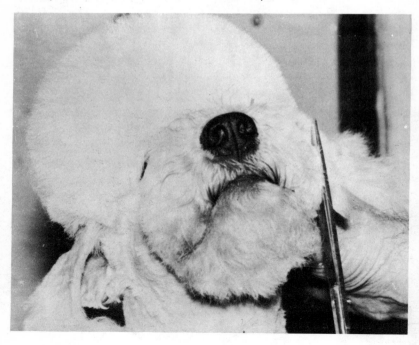

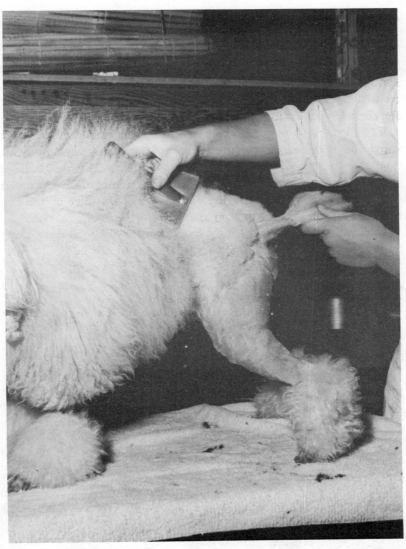

If there are to be hip rosettes on a Poodle wearing the Continental clip, they should be trimmed to perfect roundness and brushed out fully. A good trick for shaping these rosettes is to place a water glass over the hair to be left long and clippering all around it. Photo by Louise Van der Meid.

Your Poodle's face and head are the most difficult parts of the animal to clip. He can move his head much faster than his body and it is a much smaller area in which to work. The head can be controlled best when one hand of the operator holds the dog's muzzle and the other hand works the clippers. Usually, when the muzzle is to be clipped clean, the hand holding it is above the foreface with thumb and fingers curling down over the muzzle. But in clips where a moustache is to be left, such as the Royal Dutch clip, the hand should be held under the jaw with the fingers curled up around the muzzle to protect the moustache.

The Poodle's lips are particularly difficult to clip close and clean without nipping. When clipping the hair from the edge of the lip, carefully pull back the corner of the mouth with the fingers holding the muzzle to cause the lip-edge hair to bristle away from the skin.

A properly shaped pack in the English Saddle clip can be made to cover many faults. The dog should be carefully studied to determine his virtues and shortcomings and should be trimmed to accentuate the former and minimize the latter. Photo by Louise Van der Meid.

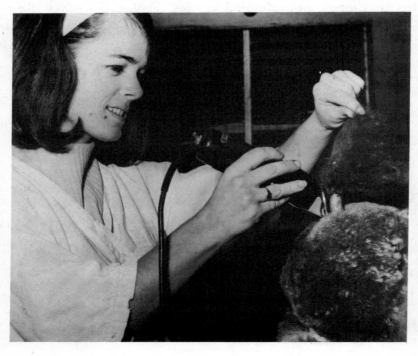

When clipping the under neck for a Dutch trim, hold the dog's head up, muzzle pointing toward the ceiling. Always keep in mind the lines of demarkation you have visualized for the clip you are endeavoring to accomplish, for once hair is cut it cannot be pasted back and you will have to wait until it has grown in again.

The Poodle's feet are a bit touchy to clip and you will find that he will attempt to pull them back when you work on them. This is one place where you will often have to cut against the grain of the hair. Remember to cut the hair that grows from between the pads at the bottom of the feet. When cutting the hair between the toes be careful not to nick the web that stretches between the toes. To trim the back feet get behind the dog so that his back is toward you. You will find this an easier way to work in that area.

The tail should be clipped halfway down and clean to where it meets the body. The tassel left at the tip should be fluffed out and then trimmed with the shears to form a ball.

To clip the underbelly, the dog, if a Toy or Miniature, should be rolled over on its back or, standing behind it as when the back feet are clipped, grasp the hind legs and lift them up so that the Poodle is standing on his front legs only, then run the clippers along the belly line.

The back is the easiest part of the Poodle to clip. When executing the Dutch clip place the flat of the blade facing toward the dog's rear and begin directly behind the head pompadour running the clipper full length of the back from the back of the skull to the tail set.

The hip and leg pompoms that identify the Continental clip can be marked on the coat with colored chalk with the first clipping so that they will be placed even on both sides of the dog.

When you have completed the job of clipping, comb the hair out and view the result from different angles to get the full effect of your handiwork. You will see the stray ends that spoil the outline and can go to work with the shears to even up and smooth the finished product.

You will probably be exhausted after the first attempt at clipping, but, when you see what you have accomplished, you will agree that the results have justified the effort. And you can bask in the knowledge that each time you clip your Poodle the task will be easier as you gain skill and sureness. Aside from this satisfaction, think of the money you saved!

THE THREE SHOW CLIPS

Poodles must wear one of three clips when exhibited in show competition: the English Saddle clip, the Continental clip, or the Puppy clip. Your Poodle may be shown in the Puppy clip until he is a year old. From that age on he will not be acceptable in the show ring unless he wears the English Saddle or Continental clip.

In America most exhibitors fancy the English Saddle clip. It is a simple clipping process to convert the Puppy clip to either the English Saddle or the Continental.

In the Puppy clip the face, feet and the bottom half of the tail are clipped clean. The tail pompom is shaped round with the shears and the hair on the head, ears, neck, body and legs is combed out and trimmed slightly with the shears to present a pleasing silhouette.

The Puppy clip may be worn by Poodles in the show ring up to their first birthday. It consists of clippered face, feet, and tail. A small amount of scissoring is allowed on the body to show the dog's basic outline.

The English Saddle clip is the most popular show clip in the United States. While it remains basically the same, varitations will appear from time to time. An example of this is the crescent behind the ruff. Many handlers will trim it much smaller than the above illustration, making it nothing more than a "kidney patch."

When the Puppy reaches show ring maturity you clip to the variations of the English Saddle clip. The face, base of tail, feet, legs and sections of body, are clipped clean and close. One pompom is left on the front legs and two on the hind legs. The blanket on the hindquarters is trimmed medium close to exhibit the close and heavy Persian lamb curl. The hair of the topknot, mane and ears is left long. The leg and tail pompoms are also left long but slightly trimmed to shape.

The Continental clip is basically the same as the English Saddle and it is easy to convert to this clip from either the Puppy or English Saddle clip. The obvious difference between the English Saddle and the Continental is the lack of the curly saddle in the latter clip.

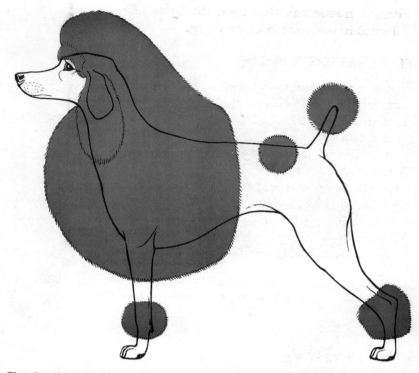

The Continental clip is the third of the approved clips for the American show ring. It differs from the English Saddle clip in that there is no saddle, but rather a rosette over the hock joint and an optional rosette over the hips. This clip is becoming increasingly popular.

Also the upper bracelet on the hind legs is deleted and a rosette added to the hip.

An important feature of all three of the show clips is the fullness of the mane. It must be combed to stand out, away from the body, to form the fluffy halo of hair around the dog that is the trademark of the breed.

Many years ago there was another approved coat type in Poodles, the Corded Poodle. The coat was allowed to grow without clipping or brushing and was oiled to prevent hair from breaking. Treated in such a manner the coat formed thin, round mats of hair which, when allowed to become long, formed a mass of ropelike cords to the floor. It was a coat fad and certainly not a very sanitary one. The odorous, matted hair that made the Corded Poodle would not be tolerated in our more enlightened age.

TWO FAVORITE CLIPS

There are two clips that seem to have become perennial favorites, one because it is a utility clip (the Kennel clip), the other because it seems to personify the basic personality of the Poodle as a breed (the Dutch clip).

The Kennel clip is easily accomplished and easy to maintain. When several or many dogs are kept in a kennel they can, in a Kennel clip, always be neat and clean appearing. Another virtue inherent in this clip is its closeness to the basic show clips. By allowing the coat to achieve a bit more fullness the Kennel clip can readily be fashioned to a Puppy, English Saddle or Continental clip.

In the Kennel clip the face, feet and lower half of the tail are

The Kennel clip is a serviceable clip for the pet Poodle and is most practical for the Poodle brood bitch.

clipped clean. The hair on the head pompom, ears and tail pompom is left long but shaped to a pleasing outline with the shears. The neck and body are clipped to approximately one inch length (longer on larger Standard Poodles), to exhibit the tight, Persian lamb curl for which the breed is noted. The hair on the legs is scissored to approximately the double length of the body hair.

The second clip seems to be a universal favorite both here and on the continent: the Royal Dutch clip. It is the most widely used clip for pets especially in the Toy and Miniature sizes and it seems a shame that it is not an accepted show ring clip in America.

To accomplish the Royal Dutch clip the feet, neck, middle body band, all of the ear except the tassel, all of the face except the moustache, the bottom half of the tail and a string along the middle of the back, are clipped close and clean. The facial "whiskers" are left unclipped and combed forward, the head pompom is trimmed to

The Royal Dutch clip is the most widely-known pet clip. Many variations of this clip exist in the United States and in Europe.

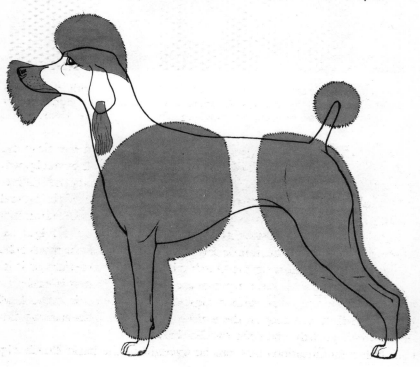

Any clip will look better if the job is finished off with scissors. A careful operator will always put some scissor work into a dog whether a show or pet clip is involved. Photo by Three Lions.

a graduated "V" on the neck. Ear tassels are left on the clean ear and are combed down. The rest of the body, which is unclipped, is trimmed with shears to remove any raggedness from the outline.

In the three Show clips there can be no innovation if the animal is to be shown, and the Kennel clip serves its purpose admirably as it is. But, in the Dutch clip, modifications can be indulged in. Many owners clean the muzzle completely, clipping off the moustache or whiskers but allowing the Dutch clip otherwise to remain as it is. Poodle owners who have a pet house dog claim that it is easier to keep the animal clean with a clipped muzzle since it keeps food particles from catching in the whiskers and water from soaking this extra hair growth when the Poodle drinks.

Other modifications that can be wrought in the basic Dutch clip

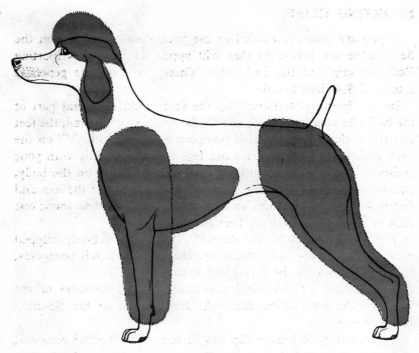

The Sporting Retriever clip is one variation of the Royal Dutch. The pet clip a Poodle is to wear is a matter of the owner's individual taste, but the dog should be trimmed in a manner most flattering to him.

is to eliminate the neck "V" and shape the head pompom round, and shape the hindquarters cut to resemble the back end of the English Saddle clip.

The Dutch clip lends itself readily to improvisation by the imaginative owner and this is a good thing. It's your dog and your clippers, so have fun.

In Europe, the ban on showing Poodles in the Royal Dutch clip has been lifted. But dogs, so clipped are at a handicap when shown against Poodles in the traditional "Lion" or Continental clip (in England the Royal Dutch is called the "modern" clip). The reason for this handicap is because Poodles shown in the classic show clips exhibit all the many virtues that are the essential necessities of a fine Poodle to a greater degree than is offered by the Royal Dutch clip.

SPORTING CLIPS

If you are sporting-minded or use your Poodle for work in the field, there are two clips that will appeal to you: the Sporting Retriever clip and the Field clip. These two clips are generally found on Standard Poodles.

In the Sporting Retriever clip the face, neck, back and part of the body are closely clipped, also the bottom half of the tail, the feet and the underbody. The head pompom is shaped to a "V" on the neck and the hair on the ears and legs trimmed slightly with your shears to present a neat outline. The middle section on the body, extending from the front legs back to the beginning of the loin and embracing the ribs to form an oval shape, is trimmed to about one inch in length to display the Persian lamb curl.

The Field clip is much simpler. The dog is closely clipped throughout, leaving only the moustache, head and tail pompoms, and ear tassels as in the Royal Dutch clip.

Modifications of the Field clip could include removal of the whiskers and leaving the ears fully feathered as in the Sporting Retriever clip.

The Sporting Retriever clip can be modified by either removing the oval, tightly curled rib cover, or allowing the Persian lamb effect to extend over the areas legitimately cut closely, with only the head and neck clipped clean.

The Poodle coat is adaptable to many kinds of clips just as the Poodle itself can become adapted to many kinds of environment and various purposes. But, no matter what clip you employ, if your dog is well groomed and well clipped it will be handsome, beautiful and stylish, as a Poodle should.

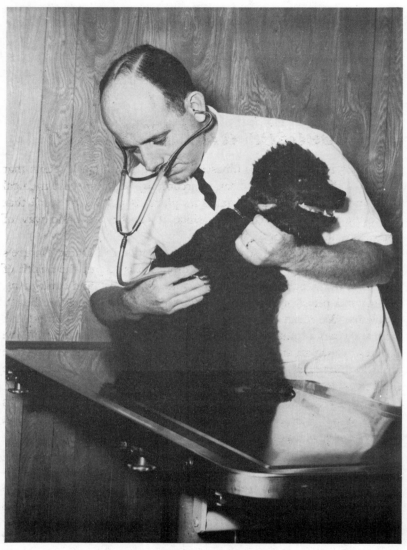

The modern small animal veterinarian stands ready, by reason of long years of experience and intensive study, to safeguard the health and add years to the lives of all dogs. New procedures and new drugs have made it possible for the veterinarian to affect cures that were completely unheard of a few years ago. Photo by Louise Van der Meid.

Chapter 14

Diseases and First Aid

The dog is heir to many illnesses, and, as with man, it seems that when one dread form has been overcome by some specific medical cure, another quite as lethal takes its place. It is held by some that this cycle will always continue, since it is nature's basic way of controlling species population.

There are, of course, several ways to circumvent Dame Nature's lethal plans. The initial step in this direction is to put the health of your dogs in the hands of one who has the knowledge and equipment, mental and physical, to competently cope with your canine health problems. We mean, of course, a modern veterinarian. Behind this man are years of study and experience and a knowledge of all the vast research, past and present, which has developed the remarkable cures and artificial immunities that have so drastically lowered the canine mortality rate as of today.

Put your trust in the qualified veterinarian and "beware of Greeks bearing gifts." Beware, too, of helpful friends who say, "I know what the trouble is and how to cure it. The same thing happened to my dog." Home doctoring by unskilled individuals acting upon the advice of unqualified "experts" has killed more dogs than distemper.

Your Poodle is constantly exposed to innumerable diseases through the medium of flying and jumping insects, helminths, bacteria, fungi, and viruses. His body develops defenses and immunities against many of these diseases, but there are many more which we must cure or immunize him against if they are not to prove fatal.

We are not qualified to give advice about treatment for the many menaces to your dog's health that exist and, by the same token, you are not qualified to treat your dog for these illnesses with the skill or knowledge necessary for success. We can only give you a resumé of modern findings on the most prevalent diseases and illnesses so that you can, in some instances, eliminate them or the causative agent yourself. Even more important, this chapter will help you recognize their symptoms in time to seek the aid of your veterinarian.

Though your dog can contract disease at any time or any place, he or she is most greatly exposed to danger when in the company of others dogs at dog shows or in a boarding kennel. Watch your dog carefully after it has been hospitalized or sent afield to be bred. Many illnesses have an incubation period, during the early stages of which the animal himself may not show the symptoms of the disease, but can readily contaminate other dogs with which he comes in contact. It is readily seen, then, that places where many dogs are gathered together, such as those mentioned above, are particularly dangerous to your dog's health.

Parasitic diseases, which we will first investigate, must not be taken too lightly, though they are the easiest of the diseases to cure. Great suffering and even death can come to your dog through these parasites that prey on him if you neglect to realize the importance of both cure and the control of reinfestation.

EXTERNAL PARASITES

The lowly flea is one of the most dangerous insects from which you must protect your dog. It carries and spreads tapeworm, heartworm and bubonic plague, causes loss of coat and weight, spreads skin disease, and brings untold misery to its poor host. These pests are particularly difficult to combat because their eggs—of which they lay thousands—can lie dormant for months, hatching when conditions of moisture and warmth are present. Thus you may think you have rid your dog (and your house) of these devils, only to find that they mysteriously reappear as weather conditions change.

When your dog has fleas, use any good commercial flea powder that contains malathion, lindane, or any similar insecticide. Pyrethrins and rotenone flea powders are excellent, but not long lasting. Dust him freely with the powder. It is not necessary to cover the dog completely, since the flea is active and will quickly reach a spot saturated with the powder and die. These compounds are also fatal to lice. DDT in liquid soap is excellent and long-potent, its effects lasting for as long as a week. Your dog's sleeping quarters as well as the animal itself should be treated. Repeat the treatment in ten days to eliminate fleas which have been newly hatched from dormant eggs. Chlorinated hydrocarbons (DDT, chlordane, dieldrin, etc.) are long acting. Organic phosphoriferous substances such as malathion, are quick killers with no lasting effect.

TICKS

There are many kinds of ticks, all of which go through similar stages in their life process. At some stage in their lives they all find it necessary to feed on blood. Luckily, these vampires are fairly easily controlled. The female of the species is much larger than the male, which will generally be found hiding under the female. Care must be taken in the removal of these pests to guard against the head's remaining embedded in the dog's skin when the body of the tick is removed. Chlorinated hydrocarbons are effective tick removers. Ether or nail-polish remover, touched to the individual tick, will cause it to relax its grip and fall off the host. The heated head of a match from which the flame has been just extinguished, employed in the same fashion, will cause individual ticks to release their hold and fall from the dog. After veterinary tick treatment, no attempt should be made to remove the pests manually, since the treatment will cause them to drop by themselves as they succumb.

MITES

There are three basic species of mites that generally infect dogs, the demodectic mange mite (red mange), the sarcoptic mange mite (white mange), and the ear mite (otodectic mange). Demodectic mange is generally recognized by balding areas on the face, cheeks, and the front parts of the foreleg, which present a moth-eaten appearance. Reddening of the skin and great irritation occurs as a result of the frantic rubbing and scratching of affected parts by the animal. Rawness and thickening of the skin follows. Not too long ago this was a dread disease in dogs, from which few recovered. It is still a persistent and not easily cured condition unless promptly diagnosed and diligently attended to.

Sarcoptic mange mites can infest you as well as your dog. The resulting disease is known as scabies. This disease very much resembles dry dermatitis, or what is commonly called "dry eczema." The coat falls out and the denuded area becomes inflamed and itches constantly.

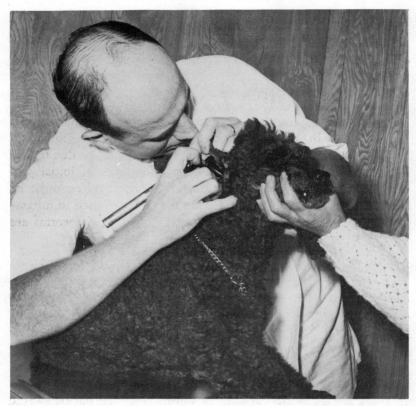

When a dog continually shakes its head and scratches at its ears it is probably suffering from an ear mite infestation. Prompt action is necessary for if this condition is neglected it can lead to ear canker.
Photo by Louise Van der Meid.

Ear mites, of course, infest the dog's ear and can be detected by an accumulation of crumbly dark brown or black wax within the ear. Shaking of the head and frequent scratching at the site of the infestation accompanied by squeals and grunting also is symptomatic of the presence of these pests. Canker of the ear is a condition, rather than a specific disease, which covers a wide range of ear infection. Canker can be initiated by ear mite infection.

All three of these conditions should be treated by your veterinarian. By taking skin scrapings or wax particles from the ear for microscopic examination, he can make an exact diagnosis and recommend specific treatment. The irritations caused by these ailments, unless immediately controlled, can result in loss of appetite and weight, and so lower your dog's natural resistance that he is open to the attack of other diseases which his bodily defenses could normally battle successfully.

INTERNAL PARASITES

It seems strange, in the light of new discovery of specific controls for parasitism, that the incidence of parasitic infestation should still be almost as great as it was years ago. This can only be due to lack of realization by the dog owner of the importance of initial prevention and control against reinfestation. Strict hygiene must be adhered to if dogs properly treated are not to be exposed to infestation immediately again. This is particularly true where worms are concerned.

1. Flea-host tapeworm. 2. Segment of tapeworm as seen in dog's stool. 3. Common roundworm. 4. Whipworm. 5. Hookworm. 6. Heartworm.

In attempting to rid our dogs of worms, we must not be swayed by amateur opinion. The so-called "symptoms" of worms may be due to many other reasons. We may see the actual culprits in the animal's stool, but even then it is not wise to worm indiscriminately. The safest method to pursue is to take a small sample of your dog's stool to your veterinarian. By a fecal analysis he can advise just what specific types of worms infest your dog and what drugs should be used to eliminate them.

Do not worm your dog because you "think" he should be wormed, or because you are advised to do so by some self-confessed "authority." Drugs employed to expel worms can prove highly dangerous to your dog if used indiscriminately and carelessly, and in many instances the same symptoms that are indicative of the presence of internal parasites can also be the signs of some other affliction.

A word here in regard to that belief that garlic will "cure" worms. Garlic is an excellent flavoring agent, favored by gourmets the world over, but it will not rid your dog of worms. Its only curative power lies in the fact that, should you use it on a housedog who has worms, the first time he pants in your face you will definitely be cured of ever attempting this psuedo-remedy again.

ROUNDWORM

These are the most common worms found in dogs and can have grave effects upon puppies, which they almost invariably infest. Potbellies, general unthriftiness, diarrhea, coughing, lack of appetite, anemia, are the symptoms. They can also cause verminous pneumonia when in the larval stage. Fecal examinations of puppy stools should be made by your veterinarian frequently if control of these parasites is to be constant. Although theoretically it is possible for small puppies to be naturally worm free, actually most puppies are born infested (larvae in the bloodstream of the bitch cross the placenta to infect the unborn pups) or contract the eggs at the mother's breast or from the surrounding environment.

The roundworm lives in the intestine and feeds on the dog's partially digested food, growing and laying eggs which are passed out in the dog's stool to be picked up by him in various ways and so cause reinfestation. The life history of all the intestinal worms is a vicious circle, with the dog the beginning and the end host. This worm is yellowish-white in color and is shaped like a common garden worm, pointed at both ends. It is usually curled when found in the stool. There are several different species of this type of worm. Some varieties are more dangerous than others. They discharge toxin within the dog, and the presence of larvae in important organs of the dog's body can cause death.

The drugs most used by kennel owners for the elimination of roundworms are N-butyl-chloride, tetrachloroethylene and the piperazines, but there are a host of other drugs, new and old, that can also do the job efficiently. With most of the worm drugs, give no food to the dog for twenty-four hours, or in the case of puppies, twenty hours, previous to the time they are given the medicine. It is absolutely essential that this starvation limit be adhered to if the drug used is tetrachloroethylene, since the existence of the slightest amount of food in the stomach or intestine can cause death. One tenth c.c. to each pound of the animal's weight up to 50 pounds is the dosage for tetrachloroethylene, followed in one hour with a milk-of-magnesia physic, never an oily physic. Food may be given two hours later. Piperazines are less toxic, and the dog can be fed normally. Large doses of the drug can be given grown dogs without danger.

HOOKWORMS

These tiny worms that live on the blood of your dog, which they get from the intestinal walls, cause severe anemia, groaning, fits, diarrhea, loss of appetite and weight, rapid breathing, and swelling of the legs. Some of the same drugs used to eradicate roundworms will also expel hookworms. Disophenol, in subcutaneous injection, is the newest and most effective hookworm treatment. Tetrachlorethylene, N-butyl-chloride and tolkuene are drugs also used for hookworms.

Good food is essential for quick recovery, with added amounts of liver and raw meat and iron tonics incorporated in the diet. Blood transfusions are often necessary if the infestation has been heavy. If one infestation follows another, a certain degree of immunity to the effects of the parasite seems to be built up by the dog. A second treatment should be given two weeks following the initial treatment.

WHIPWORMS

These small, thin whiplike worms are found in the intestines and the cecum. Those found in the intestines are reached and killed by the same drugs used in the eradication of roundworms and hookworms. Most worm medicines will kill these helminths if they reach them, but those which live in the cecum are very difficult to reach. They exude toxins which cause debilitation, anemia, and allied ills, and are probably a contributing factor in lowering the resistance to the onslaught of other infections. The usual symptoms of worm infestation are present, especially vomiting, diarrhea, and loss of weight. Phthalofyne is an effective whipworm eradicator. It can be administered by either intravenous injection or by oral tablets.

TAPEWORMS

Tapeworms are not easily diagnosed by fecal test, but are easily identified when visible in the dog's stool. The worm is composed of two distinct parts, the head and the segmented body. It is pieces of the segmented body that we see in the stools of the dog. They are usually pink or white in color and flat. The common tapeworm, which is most prevalent in our dogs, is about eighteen inches long, and the larvae are carried by the flea. The head of the worm is smaller than a pinhead and attaches itself to the intestinal wall. Contrary to general belief, the dog infested with tapeworms does not possess an enormous appetite, rather it fluctuates from good to poor. The animal shows the general signs of worm infestation. Often he squats and drags his hindquarters on the ground. This is due to tapeworm segments moving and wriggling in the lower bowels. One must be careful in diagnosing this symptom, as it may also mean that the dog is suffering from distended anal glands.

Arecolene is one of the most efficient expellers of tapeworms. Dosage is approximately one-tenth grain for every fifteen pounds of the dog's weight, administered after twenty hours of fasting. No worm medicine can be considered 100 percent effective in all cases. If one drug does not expel the worms satisfactorily, then another must be tried.

HEARTWORM

This villain inhabits the heart and is the most difficult to treat. The worm is about a foot long and literally stuffs the heart of the affected animal. It is prevalent in the southern states and has long been the curse of sporting-dog breeds. This does not signify that other dogs cannot become infected, since the worm is transmitted principally through the bite of an infected mosquito, which can fly from an infected southern canine visitor directly to another dog and do its dire deed.

The symptoms are: fatigue, gasping, coughing, nervousness, and sometimes dropsy and swelling of the extremities. Treatment for heartworms definitely must be left in the hands of your veterinarian. A wide variety of drugs are used in treatment, the most commonly employed are the arsenicals, antimony compounds, and caracide. Danger exists during cure when dying worms move to the lungs, causing suffocation, or when dead worms, in a heavily infested dog, block the small blood vessels in the heart muscles. The invading microfilariae are not discernible in the blood until nine months following introduction of the disease by the bite of the carrier mosquito.

In an article on this subject in *Field and Stream* magazine, Joe Stetson describes a controlled experiment in which caracide was employed in periodic treatments as a preventive of heartworm. The experiment was carried out over a period of eighteen months, during which time the untreated dogs became positive for heartworm and eventually died. A post mortem proved the presence of the worm. The dogs that underwent scheduled prophylaxis have been found, by blood test, to be free of circulating microfilariae and are thriving.

COCCIDIOSIS

This disease is caused by a tiny protozoan. It affects dogs of all ages, but is not dangerous to mature animals. When puppies become infected by a severe case of coccidiosis, it very often proves fatal, since it produces such general weakness and emaciation that the puppy has no defense against other invading harmful organisms. Loose and bloody stools are indicative of the presence of this disease, as is loss of appetite, weakness, emaciation, discharge from the eyes, and a fever of approximately 103 degrees. The disease is contracted directly or through flies that have come from infected quarters. Infection seems to occur over and over again, limiting the puppy's chance of recovery with each succeeding infection. The duration of the disease is about three weeks, but new infestations can stretch this period of illness on until your puppy has little chance to recover. Strict sanitation and supportive treatment of good nutrition—utilizing milk, fat, kaopectate, and bone ash with added dextrose and calcium—seem to be all that can be done in the way of treatment. Force feed the puppy if necessary. The more food that you can get into him to give him strength until the disease has run its course, the better will be his chances of recovery. Specific cures have been developed in other animals and poultry, but not as yet in dogs. Fragmentary clinical evidence would seem to indicate that sulfamethazine may give some control in canine coccidiosis.

SKIN DISEASES

Diseases of the skin in dogs are many, varied, and easily confused by the kennel owner as to category. All skin afflictions should be immediately diagnosed by your veterinarian so that treatment can begin with dispatch. Whatever drug is prescribed must be employed diligently and in quantity and generally long after surface indications of the disease have ceased to exist. A surface cure may be attained, but the infection remains buried deep in the hair follicles or skin glands, to erupt again if treatment is suspended too soon. Contrary to popular belief, diet, if well balanced and complete is, seldom the cause of skin disease. Because of his unique coat, skin diseases can be particularly acute in the Poodle.

Eczema

The word "eczema" is a much-abused word, as is the word "dermatitis." Both are used with extravagance in the identification of various forms of skin disorders. We will concern ourselves with the two most prevalent forms of so-called eczema, namely wet eczema and dry eczema, In the wet form, the skin exudes moisture and then scabs over, due to constant scratching and biting by the dog at the site of infection. The dry form manifests itself in dry patches which irritate and itch, causing great discomfort to the dog. In both instances the hair falls out and the spread of the disease is rapid. The cause of these diseases is not yet known, though many are thought to be originated by various fungi and bacteria and aggravated by flea allergic conditions and self trauma. The quickest means of bringing these diseases under control is through the application of a good skin remedy often combined with a fungicide, which your veterinarian will prescribe. An over-all dip, employing specific liquid medication, is beneficial in many cases and has a continuing curative effect over a period of days. Injectable or oral anti-inflammatory drugs are often employed as supplementary treatment.

Ringworm

This infection is caused by a fungus and is highly contagious to humans. In the dog it generally appears on the face as a round or oval spot from which the hair has fallen. It is not as often seen in long-coated dogs as it is in shorter-coated dogs. Ringworm is easily controlled by the application of iodine glycerine (fifty percent of each ingredient) or a fungicide such as girseofulvin, a definite cure for ringworm.

Acne

Your puppy will frequently display small eruptions on his belly or eyelids, paws and muzzle. The rash is caused by a bacterial infection of the skin glands and hair follicles and is not serious if treated early. Wash the affected areas with alcohol or witch hazel and apply a healing lotion or powder. Hormonal imbalances can cause specific skin conditions that are best left to the administrations of your veterinarian.

Hookworm Larvae Infection

The skin of your dog can become infected from the larvae of the hookworm acquired from muddy, hookworm-infested runs. The larvae become stuck to his coat with mud and burrow into the skin, leaving ugly raw red patches. One or two baths in warm water to which an antiseptic has been added usually cures the condition quickly.

DEFICIENCY DISEASES

These diseases, or conditions, are caused by dietary deficiencies or some condition which robs the diet of necessary ingredients. Anemia, a deficiency condition, is a shortage of hemoglobin. Hookworms, lice, and any disease that depletes the system of red blood cells, are contributory causes. A shortage or lack of specific minerals or vitamins in the diet can also cause anemia. Not so long ago, rickets was the most common of the deficiency diseases, caused by a lack of one or more of the dietary elements: vitamin D, calcium, and phosphorous. There are other types of deficiency diseases originating in dietary inadequacy and characterized by unthriftiness in one or more phases. The cure consists of supplying the missing food factors to the diet. Sometimes, even though all the necessary dietary elements are present in the food, some are destroyed by improper feeding procedure. For example, a substance in raw eggs, avertin, destroys biotin, one of the B-complex group of vitamins. Cooking will destroy the avertin in the egg white and prevent a biotin deficiency in the diet.

BACTERIAL DISEASES

In this group we find leptospirosis, tetanus, pneumonia, and many other dangerous diseases. The mortality rate is generally high in all of the bacterial diseases, and treatment should be left to your veterinarian. -

Leptospirosis

Leptospirosis is spread most frequently by the urine of infected dogs, which can infect for six months or more after the animal has recovered from the disease. Rats are the carriers of the bacterial agent that produces this disease. A dog will find a bone upon which an infected rat has urinated, chew the bone, and become infected with the disease in turn. Leptospirosis is primarily dangerous in the damage it does to the kidneys. Complete isolation of affected individuals to keep the disease from spreading and rat control of kennel areas are the chief means of control. Vaccines are employed by your veterinarian as a preventive measure. Initial diagnosis is difficult, and the disease generally makes drastic inroads before a cure is effected. It has been estimated that fully fifty percent of all dogs throughout the world have been stricken with leptospirosis at one time or another, and that in many instances the disease was not recognized for what it was. The disease produced by *Leptospira* in the blood of humans is known as Weil's disease.

Tetanus

Lockjaw bacteria produce an exceedingly deadly poison. The germs grow in the depths of a sealed-over wound where oxygen cannot penetrate. To prevent this disease, every deep wound acquired by your dog should be thoroughly cleansed and disinfected, and an antitoxin given the animal. Treatment follows the same general pattern as prevention. If the jaw locks, intravenous feeding must be given.

Tonsillitis

Inflammation of the tonsils can be either of bacterial or virus origin. It is not a serious disease in itself, but is often a symptom of other diseases. The symptoms of tonsillitis are enlarged and reddened tonsils, poor appetite, vomiting, and optic discharge. The condition usually runs its course in from five to seven days. Penicillin, aureomycin, terramycin, chloromycetin, etc., have been used with success in treatment.

Pneumonia

Pneumonia is a bacterial disease of the lungs of which the symptoms are poor appetite, optic discharge, shallow and rapid respiration. Affected animals become immune to the particular type of pneumonia from which they have recovered. Oral treatment utilizing antibiotic or sulfa drugs, combined with a pneumonia jacket of cloth or cotton padding wrapped around the chest area, seems to be standard treatment. Pneumonia is quite often associated with distemper.

VIRAL DISEASES

The dread viral diseases are caused by the smallest organisms known to man. They live in the cells and often attack the nerve tissue. The tissue thus weakened is easily invaded by many types of bacteria. Complications then set in, and it is these accompanying ills, which usually prove fatal. The secondary infections can be treated with several of the "wonder" drugs, and excellent care and nursing is necessary if the stricken animal is to survive. Your veterinarian is the only person qualified to aid your dog when a virus disease strikes. The diseases in this category include distemper, infectious hepatitis, rabies, kennel cough, and primary encephalitis—the latter actually inflammation of the brain, a condition characterizing several illnesses, particularly those of viral origin.

Distemper

Until recently a great many separate diseases had been lumped under the general heading of distemper.* In the last few years modern science has isolated a number of separate diseases of the distemper complex. Thus, with more accurate diagnosis, great strides have been made in conquering, not only distemper, but these other allied diseases. Distemper (Carre) is no longer prevalent due to successful methods of immunization, but any signs of illness in an animal not immunized may be the beginning of the disease. The symptoms are so similar to those of various other diseases that only a trained observer can diagnose correctly. Treatment consists of the use of drugs to counteract complications arising from the invasion of secondary diseases and in keeping the stricken animal warm, well fed, comfortable and free from dehydration until the disease has run its course. In many instances, even if the dog gets well, he will be left with some dreadful souvenir of the disease which will mar him for life.

The tremendous value of immunization against this viral disease cannot be exaggerated. Except for the natural resistance your animal carries against disease, it is the one means of protection you have against this killer. There have been various methods of immunization developed in the last several years, combining several vaccines in one.

* See L. F. and G. D. Whitney, *The Distemper Complex* (Orange, Conn., Practical Science Publishing Co., 1953).

Injections can be given at any age, even as early as six or eight weeks, with a booster shot when recommended by your veterinarian. They do not affect the tissues, nor do they cause any ill effects to other dogs in a kennel who come in contact with the vaccinated animal.

Infectious Hepatitis

This disease attacks dogs of all ages, but is particularly deadly to puppies. We see young puppies in the nest, healthy, bright and sturdy; suddenly they begin to vomit, and the next day they are dead of infectious hepatitis; it strikes that quickly. The disease is difficult to diagnose correctly, and there is no specific treatment that will cure it. Astute authorities claim that if an afflicted dog survives three days after the onslaught of the disease he will, in all probability, completely recover. Treatment is symptomatic and directed at supporting the functions of the ailing liver. Prevention is through vaccination. Veterinarian vaccine programs usually combine distemper, hepatitis, and often leptospirosis vaccines.

Rabies

This is the most terrible of diseases, since it knows no bounds. It is transmissible to all kinds of animals and birds, including the superior animal, man. To contract this dread disease, the dog must be bitten by a rabid animal or the rabies virus must enter the body through a broken skin surface. The disease incubation period is governed by the distance of the virus' point of entry to the brain. The closer the point of entry is to the brain, the quicker the disease manifests itself. We can be thankful that rabies is not nearly as prevalent as is supposed by the uninformed. Restlessness, excitability, perverted appetite, character reversal, wildness, drowsiness, loss of acuteness of senses, and of feeling in some instances, foaming at the mouth, and many other lesser symptoms come with the onslaught of this disease. Diagnosis by trained persons of a portion of the brain is conceded to be the only way of determining whether an animal died of rabies or of one of the distemper complex diseases. Very little has been done in introducing drugs or specifics that can give satisfaction in combatting this disease, perhaps evaluation of the efficacy of such products is almost impossible with a disease so rare and difficult to diagnose.

Quarantine, such as that pursued in England, even of six-months' duration, is still not the answer to the rabies question, though it is undeniably effective. It is, however, not proof positive. Recently a dog on arriving in England was held in quarantine for the usual six months. The day before he was to be released to his owners, the attendant noticed that he was acting strangely. He died the next day. Under examination his brain showed typical inclusion bodies, establishing the fact that he had died of rabies. This is a truly dangerous disease that can bring frightful death to animal or man. It should be the duty of every dog owner to protect his dog, himself, his family, and neighbors from even the slight risk that exists of contracting rabies by having his dog immunized. In many states immunization is compulsory.

FITS

Fits in dogs are symptoms of diseases rather than illness itself. They can be caused by the onslaught of any number of diseases, including worms, distemper, epilepsy, primary encephalitis, poisoning, etc. Running fits can also be traced to dietary deficiencies. The underlying reason for the fits, or convulsions, must be diagnosed by your veterinarian and the cause treated.

DIARRHEA

Diarrhea, a loose, watery movement, is often a symptom of one of many other diseases. But if, on taking your dog's temperature, you find there is no fever, it is quite possible the condition has been caused by either a change of diet, of climate or water, or even by a simple intestinal disturbance. A tightening agent such as Kaopectate should be given. Water should be withheld and corn syrup, dissolved in boiled milk, substituted to prevent dehydration in the patient. Feed hard-boiled eggs, boiled milk, beef, boiled white rice, cracker, kibbles, or dog biscuits. Add a tablespoonful of bone ash (not bone meal) to the diet. If the condition is not corrected within two or three days, if there is an excess of blood passed in the stool, or if signs of other illness become manifest, don't delay a trip to your veterinarian.

CONSTIPATION

If the dog's stool is so hard that it is difficult for him to pass it and he strains and grunts during the process, then he is obviously constipated. The cause of constipation is generally one of diet.

Bones and dog biscuits, given abundantly, can cause this condition, as can any of the items of diet mentioned as treatment for diarrhea. Chronic constipation can result in hemorrhoids which, if persistent, must be removed by surgery. The cure for constipation and its accompanying ills is the introduction of laxative food elements into the diet. Stewed tomatoes, buttermilk, skim milk, whey, bran, alfalfa meal, and various fruits can be fed and a bland physic given. Enemas can bring quick relief. Once the condition is alleviated, the dog should be given a good balanced diet, avoiding all types of foods that will produce constipation.

EYE AILMENTS

The eyes are not only the mirror of the soul, they are also the mirror of many kinds of disease. Discharge from the eyes is one of the many symptoms warning of most internal viral, helminthic, and bacterial diseases. Of the ailments affecting the eye itself, the most usual are: glaucoma, which seems to be a hereditary disease; pink eye, a strep infection; cataracts, opacity of the lens in older dogs; corneal opacity, such as follows some cases of infectious hepatitis; and teratoma or tumors. Mange, fungus, inturned lids, and growths on the lid are other eye ailments. The wise procedure is to consult your veterinarian for specific treatment.

When the eyes show a discharge from reasons other than those that can be labeled "ailment," such as irritation from dust, wind, or sand, they should be washed with warm water on cotton or a soft cloth. After gently washing the eyes, an ophthalmic ointment combining a mild anesthetic and antiseptic can be utilized. Butyn sulphate, one percent yellow oxide of mercury, and five percent sulphathiazole ointment are all good. Boric acid seems to be falling out of favor as an ophthalmic antiseptic. The liquid discharged by the dog's tear ducts is a better antiseptic, and much cheaper.

ANAL GLANDS

If your dog consistently drags his rear parts on the ground or bites this area, the cause is probably impacted anal glands. These glands, which are located on each side of the anus, should be periodically cleared by squeezing. The job is not a nice one, and can be much more effectively done by your veterinarian. Unless these glands are kept reasonably clean, infection can become housed in this site, resulting in the formation of an abscess which will need surgical care. Dogs that get an abundance of exercise seldom need the anal glands attended to.

The many other ailments which your dog is heir to, such as cancer, rupture, heart disease, fractures, and the results of accidents, etc., must all be diagnosed and tended to by your veterinarian. When you go to your veterinarian with a sick dog, always remember to bring along a sample of his stool for analysis. Many times samples of his urine are needed too. Your veterinarian is the only one qualified to treat your dog for disease, but protection against disease is, to a great extent, in the hands of the dog's owner. If those hands are capable, a great deal of pain and misery for both dog and owner can be eliminated. Death can be cheated, investment saved, and veterinary bills kept to a minimum. A periodic health check by your veterinarian is a wise investment.

ADMINISTERING MEDICATION

Some people seem to have ten thumbs on each hand when they attempt to give medicine to their dog. They become agitated and approach the task with so little sureness that their mood is communicated to the patient, increasing the difficulties presented. Invite calmness and quietness in the patient by emanating these qualities yourself. Speak to the animal in low, easy tones, petting him slowly, quieting him down in preparation. The administration of medicine should be made without fuss and as though it is some quiet and private new game between you and your dog.

At the corner of your dog's mouth there is a lip pocket perfect for the administering of liquid medicine if used correctly. Have the animal sit, then raise his muzzle so that his head is slanted upward looking toward the sky. Slide two fingers in the corner of his mouth where the upper and lower lip edges join, pull gently outward, and you have a pocket between the cheek flesh and the gums. Into this pocket pour the liquid medicine at the rate of approximately two tablespoonfuls at a time for a full-grown Standard Poodle. Keep his head up, and the liquid will run from the pocket into his throat and he will swallow it. Continue this procedure until the complete dose has been given. This will be easier to accomplish if the medicine has been spooned into a small bottle. The bottle neck, inserted into the lip pocket, is tipped, and the contents drained at the ratio mentioned before·

To give pills or capsules, the head of the patient must again be raised with muzzle pointing upward. With one hand, grasp the cheeks of the dog just behind the lip edges where the teeth come together on the inside of the mouth. With the thumb on one side and the fingers on the other, press inward as though squeezing. The lips are pushed against the teeth, and the pressure of your fingers forces the mouth open. The dog will not completely close his mouth, since doing so would cause him to bite his lips. With your other hand, insert the pill in the patient's mouth as far back on the base of the tongue as you can, pushing it back with your second finger. Withdraw your hand quickly, allow the dog to close his mouth, and hold it closed with your hand, but not too tightly. Massage the dog's throat and watch for the tip of his tongue to show between his front teeth, signifying the fact that the capsule or pill has been swallowed.

In taking your dog's temperature, an ordinary rectal thermometer is adequate. It must be first shaken down, then dipped in vaseline, and inserted into the rectum for approximately three-quarters of its length. Allow it to remain there for no less than a full minute, restraining the dog from sitting completely during that time. When withdrawn, it should be wiped with a piece of cotton, read, then washed in alcohol—never hot water. The arrow on most thermometers at 98.6 degrees indicates normal human temperature and should be disregarded. Normal temperature for your grown dog is approximately 101 degrees; normal puppy temperature varies between $101\frac{1}{2}$ to 102 degrees. Excitement can raise the temperature, so it is best to take a reading only after the dog is calm.

In applying an ophthalmic ointment to the eye, simply pull the lower lid out, squeeze a small amount of ointment into the pocket thus produced, and release the lid. The dog will blink, and the ointment will spread over the eye.

Should you find it necessary to give your dog an enema, employ an ordinary human-size bag and rubber hose. For a Standard a catheter is not necessary (but should be used in the proper size for Miniatures and Toys). Simply grease the tip with vaseline and insert it well into the rectum. The bag should be held high for a constant flow of water. A quart of warm soapy water or plain water with a tablespoonful of salt makes an efficient enema. Less will be required for Miniatures and Toys.

FIRST AID

Emergencies quite frequently occur which make it necessary for you to care for the dog yourself until veterinary aid is available. Quite often emergency help by the owner can save the dog's life or lessen the chance of permanent injury. A badly injured animal, blinded to all else but abysmal pain, often reverts to the primitive wanting only to be left alone with his misery. Injured, panic-stricken, not recognizing you, he might attempt to bite when you wish to help him. Under the stress of fright and pain, this reaction is normal in animals. A muzzle can easily be slipped over his foreface, or a piece of bandage or strip of cloth can be fashioned into a muzzle by looping it around the dog's muzzle, crossing it under the jaws, and bringing the two ends around in back of the dog's head and tying them. Snap a leash onto his collar as quickly as possible to prevent him from running away and hiding. If it is necessary to lift him, grasp him by the neck, getting as large a handful of skin as you can, as high up on the neck as possible. Hold tight and he won't be able to turn his head far enough around to bite. Lift him by the hold you have on his neck until he is far enough off the ground to enable you to encircle his body with your other arm and support him or carry him.

Every dog owner should have handy a first-aid kit specifically for the use of his dog. It should contain a thermometer, surgical scissors, rolls of three-inch and six-inch bandage, a roll of one-inch adhesive tape, a package of surgical cotton, a jar of vaseline, enema equipment, bulb syringe, ten c.c. hypodermic syringe, flea powder, skin remedy, tweezers, ophthalmic ointment, paregoric, kaopectate, peroxide of hydrogen, merthiolate, a good antiseptic powder, alcohol, ear remedy, aspirin, milk of magnesia, castor oil, mineral oil, dressing salve.

I have prepared two charts for your reference, one covering general first-aid measures and the other a chart of poisons and antidotes. Remember that, in most instances, these are emergency measures, not specific treatments, and are designed to help you in aiding your dog until you can reach your veterinarian.

FIRST-AID CHART

Emergency	Treatment	Remarks
	Automobile, treat for shock. If gums are white, indicates probable internal injury.	
Accidents	Wrap bandage tightly around body until it forms a sheath. Keep very quiet until veterinarian comes.	Call veterinarian immediately.
Bee stings	Give paregoric, 2 teaspoonfuls for grown Standard, or aspirin to ease pain. If in state of shock, treat for same.	Call veterinarian for advice.
Bites (animal)	Tooth wounds: area should be shaved and antiseptic solution flowed into punctures with eye dropper. Iodine, merthiolate, etc., can be used. If badly bitten or ripped, take dog to your veterinarian for treatment.	If superficial wounds become infected after first aid, consult veterinarian.
Burns	Apply strong, strained tea to burned area, followed by covering of vaseline.	Unless burn is very minor, consult veterinarian immediately.
Broken bones	If break involves a limb, fashion splint to keep immobile. If ribs, pelvis, shoulder, or back involved, keep dog from moving until professional help comes.	Call veterinarian immediately.
Choking	If bone, wood, or any foreign object can be seen at back of mouth or throat, remove with fingers. If object can't be removed or is too deeply imbedded or too far back in throat, rush to veterinarian immediately.	
Cuts	Minor cuts: allow dog to lick and cleanse. If not within his reach, clean cut with peroxide, then apply merthiolate. Severe cuts: apply pressure bandage to stop bleeding—a wad of bandage over wound and bandage wrapped tightly over it. Take to veterinarian.	If cut becomes infected or needs suturing, consult veterinarian.
Dislocations	Keep dog quiet and take to veterinarian at once.	
Drowning	Artificial respiration. Lay dog on his side, push with hand on his ribs, release quickly. Repeat every 2 seconds. Treat for shock.	

234

Electric shock	Artificial respiration. Treat for shock.	Call veterinarian immediately.
Heat stroke	Quickly immerse the dog in cold water until relief is given. Give cold water enema. Or lay dog flat and pour cold water over him, turn electric fan on him, and continue pouring cold water as it evaporates.	Cold towels pressed against abdomen and back of head aid in reducing temp. quickly if quantity of water not available.
Porcupine quills	Tie dog up, hold him between knees, and pull all quills out with pliers. Don't forget tongue and inside of mouth.	See veterinarian to remove quills too deeply imbedded.
Shock	Cover dog with blanket. Allow him to rest and soothe with voice and hand.	Alcoholic beverages are NOT a stimulant. Bring to veterinarian.
Poisonous snake bite	Cut deep X over fang marks. Drop potassium permanganate into cut. Apply tourniquet above bite if on foot or leg.	Apply first aid only if a veterinarian or a doctor can't be reached.

TREATMENT FOR POISON

The important thing to remember when your dog is poisoned is that prompt action is imperative. Administer an emetic immediately. Mix hydrogen peroxide and water in equal parts. Force eight to ten tablespoonfuls of this mixture down your dog, or up to twelve tablespoonfulls (this dosage for a fully grown Standard, 6 tablespoonsful for Miniature and 2 or 3 for Toy). In a few minutes he will regurgitate his stomach contents. Once this has been accomplished, call your veterinarian. If you know the source of the poison and the container which it came from is handy, you will find the antidote on the label. Your veterinarian will prescribe specific drugs and advise on their use.

The symptoms of poisoning include trembling, panting, intestinal pain, vomiting, slimy secretion from mouth, convulsions, coma. All these symptoms are also prevalent in other illnesses, but if they appear and investigation leads you to believe that they are the result of poisoning, act with dispatch as described above.

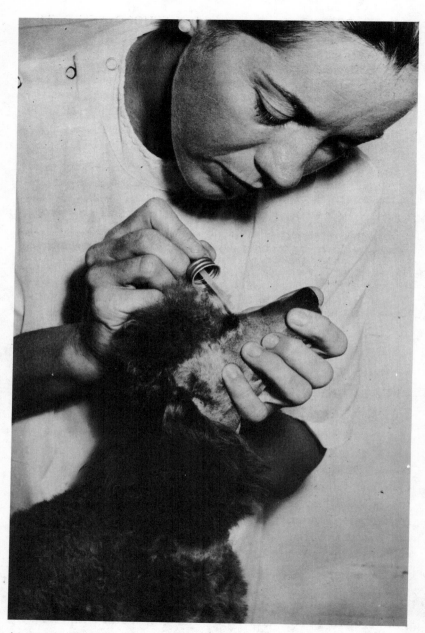

Any unusual discharge from a dog's eyes should be checked out at once. Most irritations can be corrected with the use of a mild solution designed for the purpose of eye care. Photo by Louise Van der Meid.

POISON	HOUSEHOLD ANTIDOTE
ACIDS	Bicarbonate of soda
ALKALIES	Vinegar or lemon juice
(cleansing agents)	
ARSENIC	Epsom salts
HYDROCYANIC ACID	Dextrose or corn syrup
(wild cherry; laurel leaves)	
LEAD	Epsom salts
(paint pigments)	
PHOSPHORUS	Peroxide of hydrogen
(rat poison)	
MERCURY	Eggs and milk
THEOBROMINE	Phenobarbital
(cooking chocolate)	
THALLIUM	Table salt in water
(bug poisons)	
FOOD POISONING	Peroxide of hydrogen, followed by enema
(garbage, etc.)	
STRYCHNINE	Sedatives. Phenobarbital, Nembutal.
DDT	Peroxide and enema

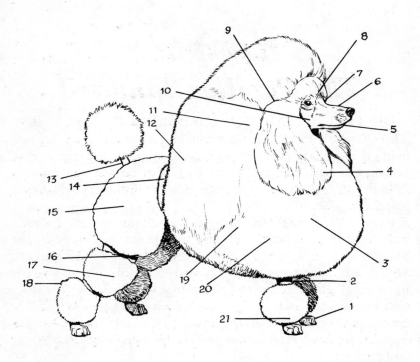

External Features of the Poodle.

1.	Feet	11.	Neck
2.	Forelegs	12.	Back
3.	Chest	13.	Tail
4.	Ear Leather	14.	Loin
5.	Lips	15.	Thigh
6.	Muzzle	16.	Stifle
7.	Eye	17.	Second Thigh
8.	Skull	18.	Hocks
9.	Ear	19.	Ribbing
10.	Cheek	20.	Elbow
	21.	Pastern	

Chapter 15

The Poodle Standard

GENERAL APPEARANCE, CARRIAGE AND CONDITION: That of a very active, intelligent and elegant-looking dog, squarely built, well-proportioned, moving soundly and carrying himself proudly. Properly clipped in the traditional fashion and carefully groomed, the Poodle has about him an air of distinction and dignity peculiar to himself.

HEAD AND EXPRESSION: (*a*) Skull: moderately rounded, with a slight but definite stop. Cheek-bones and muscles flat. Muzzle: long, straight and fine, with slight chiseling under the eyes. Strong without lippiness. The chin definite enough to preclude snipiness. Teeth white, strong and with a scissors bite. Nose sharp with well-defined nostrils. (*b*) Eyes: set far apart, very dark, full of fire and intelligence, oval in appearance. (*c*) Ears: set low and hanging close to the head. The leather should be long, wide and heavily feathered.

NECK AND SHOULDERS: Neck well proportioned, strong and long to admit of the head being carried high and with dignity. Skin snug at throat. The neck should rise from strong muscular shoulders which slope back from their point of angulation at the upper foreleg to the withers.

BODY: The chest deep and moderately wide. The ribs well sprung and braced up. The back short, strong and slightly hollowed, the loins short, broad and muscular. (Bitches may be slightly longer in back than dogs.)

TAIL: Straight, set on rather high, docked, but of sufficient length to insure a balanced outline. It should be carried up and in a gay manner.

LEGS: The forelegs straight from the shoulder, parallel and with bone and muscle in proportion to size of dog. The pasterns should be strong. The hind legs very muscular, stifles well bent and hocks well let down. The thigh should be well developed, muscular and showing width in the region of the stifle to insure strong and graceful action. The four feet should turn neither in nor out. Feet: Rather small and oval in shape. Toes arched, close and cushioned on thick, hard pads.

COAT: Quality: very profuse, of harsh texture and dense throughout.

CLIP: A Poodle may be shown in the "Puppy" clip or in the traditional "Continental" clip or the "English Saddle" clip. A Poodle under a year old may be shown in the "Puppy" clip with the coat long except the face, feet and base of tail, which should be shaved. Dogs one year old or older must be shown in either the "Continental" clip or "English Saddle" clip.

In the "Continental" clip the hindquarters are shaved with pompoms on hips (optional). The face, feet, legs and tail are shaved leaving bracelets on the hind legs, puffs on the forelegs and a pompom at the end of the tail. The rest of the body must be left in full coat.

In the "English Saddle" clip the hindquarters are covered with a short blanket of hair except for a curved shaved area on the flank and two shaved bands on each hind leg. The face, feet, forelegs and tail are shaved leaving puffs on the forelegs and a pompom at the end of the tail. The rest of the body must be left in full coat.

COLOR: The coat must be an even and solid color at the skin. In blues, grays, silvers, browns, cafe-au-laits, apricots and creams the coats may show varying shades of the same color. This is frequently present in the somewhat darker feathering of the ears and in the tipping of the ruff. While clear colors are definitely preferred such natural variation in the shading of the coat is not to be considered a fault. Brown and cafe-au-lait Poodles have liver-colored noses, eye-rims and lips, dark toenails and dark amber eyes. Black, blue, gray, silver, apricot, cream and white Poodles have black noses, eye-rims and lips, black or self-colored toenails and very dark eyes. In the apricots while black is preferred, liver-colored noses, eye-rims and lips, self-colored toenails and amber eyes are permitted but are not desirable.

GAIT: A straightforward trot with light springy action. Head and tail carried high. Forelegs and hind legs should move parallel turning neither in nor out. Sound movement is essential.

SIZE

STANDARD: The Standard Poodle is over 15 inches at the withers. Any Poodle which is 15 inches or less in height shall be disqualified from competition as a Standard Poodle.

MINIATURE: The Miniature Poodle is 15 inches or under at the withers, with a minimum height in excess of 10 inches. Any Poodle which is over 15 inches, or 10 inches or less at the withers shall be disqualified from competition as a Miniature Poodle.

TOY: The Toy Poodle is 10 inches or under at the withers. Any Poodle which is more than 10 inches at the withers shall be disqualified from competition as a Toy Poodle.

VALUE OF POINTS

General appearance, carriage and condition	20
Head, ears, eyes and expression	20
Neck and shoulders	10
Body and tail	15
Legs and feet	15
Coat—color and texture	10
Gait	10
Total	100

MAJOR FAULTS

Eyes: round in appearance, protruding, large or very light. Jaws: undershot, overshot or wry mouth. Cowhocks. Feet: flat or spread. Tail: set low, curled or carried over the back. Shyness.

DISQUALIFICATIONS

Parti-colors: The coat of a parti-colored dog is not an even solid color at the skin but is variegated in patches of two or more colors. Any type of clip other than those listed in section on coat.

Any size over or under the limits specified in section on size.

Approved July 14, 1959

Chapter 16

Discussion of the Poodle Standard

A standard is a written analysis of a breed. The essence of its combined perfections presenting to the reader a word picture of the perfect dog toward which the fancier must strive in his breeding program. In its entirety, the standard disciplines in selection and rejection toward an ethical center or objective, which is the betterment of the breed.

Standards can be too short or too vague, omitting succinct details that differentiate a particular breed from all other breeds. A standard can also be too long and rambling, confusing the reader by its sheer bulk. It is the author's considered opinion that the Poodle standard errs on the side of brevity. It could be longer and more precise in several sections.

The most obvious omission when studying the Poodle standard is the lack of a section on temperament and character. Only in "Major faults," is any reference made to temperament and there it lists only the one word, "Shyness," as a major fault. What about other vagaries in temperament such as over-sharpness or over-aggressiveness, dullness, quarrelsomeness, viciousness, aloofness?

Here we have a breed whose sole purpose is basically to be the close companion of the human race, to live with and share the lives of its master and mistress and their family. In this category the temperament, character and personality of the Poodle must be absolute and without variance. Yet in the "Value Of Points" section of the official standard no score at all is allotted to temperament.

Off-color or parti-color coats, and sizes other than those listed in the official standard are disqualifications, and these are reasonable rejections considering the official standard and its reason for existence. But so should vital faults of temperament be considered disqualifying

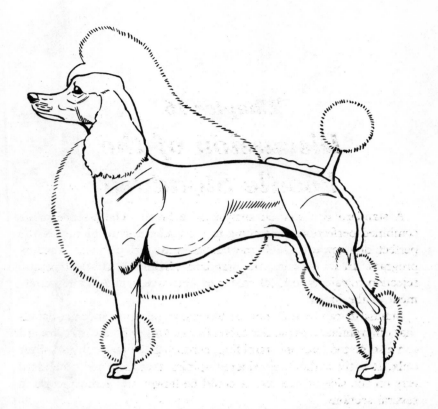

Faulty Specimen. Dish faced. Too long in body. Roached back. Too long in loin. Poor angulation. High in hock. Shoulders too far forward. Mutton withers. Shallow in body.

faults, for without proper temperament the basic reason for the Poodle's existence as a breed is gone. This is what has given the Poodle individuality and allowed the breed to prosper for centuries, this quick intelligence, this eagerness to please, this ability to do so many things well and gaily, all these many facets of intelligence and individual Poodle character and personality that have fashioned the breed's temperament.

Again referring to the point evaluation in the official standard, 40 points are allotted to the body, legs and feet, neck and shoulders, and a full half of that number, 20 points, to head, ears, eyes and expression. Granted that the head of the Poodle is distinctive and marks type and intelligence in the breed, the point evaluation is yet not just. The body and its accessories, of the Poodle or any breed,

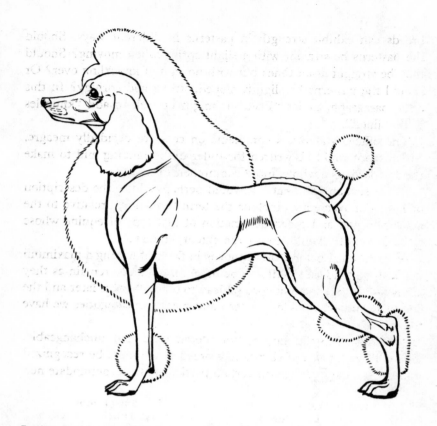

Faulty Specimen. Wet in neck. Sway back. Tail set too low. Over angulated and sickle hocked. Hare feet. Soft pasterns. Apple domed. Short in neck. Too fine-boned.

should have at least a 50% evaluation in the standard. To allow less leads to a future of physical unsoundness in the breed.

In the section labelled "Body," no mention at all is made of the Poodle's shoulder, how it should be set on, where it should be set on, and the degree of angulation it should possess to enable the dog to move correctly. In that same paragraph, referring to the ribs, the words "and braced up" have little meaning. Here too, the back is described as "slightly hollowed", a statement that lends itself to degrees in interpretation and could, as an end result, lead to weak and unsound backs.

In the segment dedicated to the Poodle's legs we find the statement, "The pasterns should be strong." This is vague since different breeds can exhibit strength in pasterns in different ways. Should the pasterns be straight with a slight spring when moving? Should they be straight at all times but with no sign of knuckling over? Or should the pasterns be slightly sloped, strong and springy? In this same paragraph, under "Feet," it might be well to add "knuckles well defined".

The official standard's comments on coat are decidedly meagre. Much more could be written for fuller understanding and to make the standard, as a whole, more comprehensible.

In the section on "Gait," it would perhaps add to the description of Poodle movement to include the term "hackney," relative to the associated gait and breed designation of that type of equine whose gait the Poodle should, to a large extent, emulate.

As mentioned before, the author is in favor of adding a maximum height for Standard Poodles. The other sizes should remain as they are for to change them now could lead to other changes later and the complete and eventual loss of the convenient size categories we have today.

A standard should not be considered rigid and unchangeable. Time brings faults and virtues to a breed which must be recognized and the standard changed in certain particulars to accommodate new

1. Cowhocks.   2. Barrel rear.

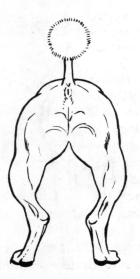

values. Since the standard is a yardstick for the show ring and the breeder, evaluation of new trends should be qualified not only by cosmetic application but by genetic implication as well. Thus faults which are of an inheritable nature should be penalized far more severely than those which are transient.

In the show ring each dog is judged, both in comparison to the animals in competition and as an individual to be evaluated against the breed standard. The basic reason for the dog show, the object in gathering together representative animals in open competition, seems to have been mislaid in the headlong pursuit for ribbons, trophies and points. Granted that consistent winning leads to self satisfaction, kennel popularity and more profitable puppy sales and stud fees, these are not, essentially, the reason for the dog show.

The graded selection of various dogs according to individual quality by a competent, unbiased judge enables earnest breeders to weigh and evaluate their own breeding procedures and the products of other breedings and strains. It gives them an idea of which breeding lines and individual animals can act as correctives to the faults inherent in their own breeding. Here the yardstick of the official standard is used to measure the defects or virtues of individual dogs and of the breed as a whole for the edification of both the knowing breeder and the novice. This is what dog shows are for primarily.

Essentially the judge should be an intermediary between the

1. East and west. Pinched front.   2. Toeing in. Loaded Shoulder.

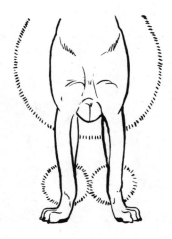 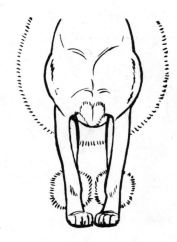

present and the future, because his (or her) decisions shape the trends for better or for worse. If these trends lead to undesirable results, there will be deterioration instead of an ever closer approach to the breed ideal. The judge is a sounding board, a calculator of degrees of excellence, an instrument for computing worth. The judge can, with every assignment, give something of enduring value toward breed improvement.

Though there are times when the judge may be at fault, we must never forget that there are more times when the exhibitor's evaluation of the judge's placings are faulty. It is difficult to be truly objective about your own dog, and too many exhibitors know too little about their breed to indulge in such criticism. It is also easy to criticize placings from the comfort of ringside. Ringsiders seldom have the opportunity to go over the dog as the judge does, to find and to see the small faults or virtues that dictate the judge's placings. Judging is not an easy task. It does not generally lead to long and cozy friendships, for once the judge steps into the ring to begin his assignment, he is no longer an individual but becomes the impartial, wholly objective instrument of the standard.

If there are judges who are really not capable of true or impartial judging, then they should not be allowed to judge by those interested in the breed. But judges, breeders, exhibitors and novices should all have the benefit of a Poodle standard that is as exact and complete in scope as the parent club can possibly make it, for it, the standard, is the only guide toward the breed ideal.

Chapter 17
The Future

What does the future hold for the Poodle breed? We are not seers so we cannot predict the future. We can only review what has gone before and refrain from repeating the mistakes of the past and present and so try to find advancement in the time to come.

Since the days of the breed's beginning we have seen it rise to the heights of popularity and then slip downward into almost obscurity. Those times of disfavor were not due to any lack of true merit in the breed itself. Rather they were the result of changes in fashion, for in dogs, as you who read this well know, styles change with the abruptness, and often the absurdity, of fashion.

The Poodle has now reached the rarest heights of popularity. The breed will not remain there overlong, no breed ever does, and it is best, considering all things, that it does not. But I do not think that it will never slide too far down the ladder again. The wonderful qualities of the breed have become too well known and too widely acclaimed to make the loss of prestige too much of a menace to reckon with in the future.

Yet the very popularity that has brought the Poodle to the top can weave the material to trip and bring about the breed's downfall. Too many transients reaching for the quick dollar, too many camp followers on the path to a breed's acclaim, can move in the wake of its popularity, breeding worthless stock through ignorance or for rapid profit. It is this stock, mere caricatures of the breed as we know and love it, that can, if allowed to continue and spread leaving enough poor specimens to constitute a large segment of deterioration in the breed, that can topple the Poodle from its deserved eminence.

Kennels born and based on monetary reward rather than breeding achievement can do terrible harm to any breed, including the Poodle. The superb intelligence and charming traits of mischievous gaiety that are the breed's inheritance will, if possible, be bred out

Ch. Tambourine de la Fontaine, owned by Alekai Kennels. Well-bred, typical Poodles such as this one should always be the breeder's chief aim. It is only by breeding and showing the best that is available that the Poodle can continue to maintain its high place among dog breeds. Photo by Evelyn Shafer.

of the Poodle in such establishments. For intelligent animals are a nuisance to the money breeder, freeing themselves from their kennels and indulging in innumerable activities that try the patience of the breeder to whom animals are dollar signs, not dogs.

Earnest breeders can aid in keeping the Poodle in the forefront of purebred dogs by spaying bitches that are not up to type mentally or physically, and stud dog owners should refuse to breed their good studs to bitches that are not good and true representatives of the breed.

Novices coming into the fold must be aided by experienced fanciers to thoroughly understand the breed. They must be guided into the proper paths so that they will help to perpetuate all those wonderful qualities, the charm, the verve, and the gay intelligence, that are part of the grand breed we call Poodles.

The author has mentioned before that he has seen Poodles in all parts of the globe. Yes, like the Romans, the Poodle has spread throughout the world (and unlike the Romans) to be cherished and loved by all peoples of all nations and creeds, a symbol of the universal dog.

Good publicity for the breed must be promulgated and the truth of the Poodle's many virtues aired. Field trials for Poodles can be arranged so that a sport-conscious public can see the breed perform as a gundog, thus adding another dimension to the Poodle's popularity and desirability.

In the final analysis the future of the Poodle is up to you, the owners and breeders. You must carry the responsibility for molding the future of the breed. New theories are being advanced, new techniques and new discoveries are constantly being made in the many fields of scientific endeavor. Never-ending research uncovers new concepts in canine medicine, nutrition, physiology, psychology and genetics. Immunities and cures are in the process of development which will destroy diseases that today take their tolls. Old problems are being met and defeated through the microscope and in testing kennels. A new future is opening up to those of us interested in dogs and the many facets of their being. We must face this future with open minds and tolerance. We must learn to understand new concepts and avoid harking back blindly to the unfounded legends and incomplete knowledge of the past.

In you, the breeder, is vested the power to fashion heredity, to

Ch. Fieldstream's Valentine, owned by Mrs. Audrey Watts Kelch.
Photo by Evelyn Shafer.

mold life. Yes, in your hands and head lies the power that creates life and change, that brings special-life forms into being. You can design a pattern of heredity with every breeding you make. You can fashion living creatures, Poodles, into a design of your own choosing. If you use this power, this ability well, the breed will prosper and the future of the Poodle will be assured.

Beyond the last words written in these pages are many more, many new words that the future will write, continuing and improving upon what you have read here. Anticipate these words, look for them and, when you find them, use them to the fullest extent, for they too will be a part of the future of the grandest breed of dog on earth, the Poodle.

The End

Bibliography

Arenas, N., and Sammartino, R., "*Le Cycle Sexuel de la Chienne*." *Etude Histol Bull. Histol. Appl. Physiol. et Path.*, 16:299 (1939).

Ash, E. C., *Dogs: Their History and Development*, 2 vols., London, 1927.

Anrep, G. V., "Pitch Discrimination in the Dog." *J. Physiol.*, 53-376-85 (1920).

Barrows, W. M., *Science of Animal Life*. New York, World Book Co., 1927.

Burns, Marca, 1952. The Genetics of the Dog, Comm., Agri. Bur., Eng. 122 pp.

Castle, W. E., *Genetics and Eugenics*, 4th ed. Cambridge, Mass., Harvard University Press, 1930.

Darwin, C., *The Variation of Animals and Plants Under Domestication*, New York, D. Appleton Co., 1890.

Davenport, C. B., *Heredity in Relations to Eugenics*. New York, Henry Holt & Co., Inc., 1911.

Dorland, W. A. N., A.M., M.D., F.A.C.S., *The Ameircan Illustrated Medical Dictionary*. Philadelphia, W. B. Saunders Co., 1938.

Duncan, W. C., *Dog Training Made Easy*. Boston, Little, Brown & Co., 1940.

Dunn, L. C., and Dobzhansky, T., *Heredity, Race and Society*. New York, New American Library of World Literature, 1946.

Elliot, David D., *Training Gun Dogs to Retrieve*. New York, Henry Holt & Co., 1952.

Evans, H. M., and Cole, H. H., "An Introduction to the Study of the Oestrus Cycle of the Dog." *Mem. Univ. Cal.*, Vol. 9, No. 2.

Hart, E. H., "Artificial Insemination." *Your Dog* (March, 1948).

———— "The Judging Situation." *Your Dog* (March, 1948).

———— 1950. Doggy Hints. Men Mg. Zenith Pub. Co.

———— *This Is The Puppy*, T.F.H. Publications, 1962.

———— *How To Clip Your Poodle*, T.F.H. Publications, 1964.

———— *Dogs Of All Breeds*, T.F.H. Publications, 1965.

Hermansson, K. A., "Artificial Impregnation of the Dog." *Svensk. Vet. Tidshr.*, 39:382 (1934).

Kelly, G. L., and Whitney, L. F., Prevention of Conception in Bitches by Injections of Estrone. *J. Ga. Med. Assoc.*, 29:7 (1940).

Kraus, C., "*Beitrag zum Prostatakrebs und Kryptorchismus des Hundes.*" *Frankfurter Zeitsch. Path.*, 41:405 (1931).

Krushinsky, L. A., "A Study of the Phenogenetics of Behaviour Characters in Dogs." *Biol. Journ. T.*, VII, No. 4, Inst. Zool., Moscow State Univ. (1938).

Laughlin, H. H., "Racing Capacity of Horses." Dept. of Genetics 37-73. Yearbook, Carn. Inst., No. 30, *The Blood Horse*, 1931.

MacDowell, E. C., "Heredity of Behaviour in Dogs." Dept. of Genetics, *Yearbook*, Carn. Inst., No. 20, 1921, 101-56.

Nagel, W. A., *Der Farbensinn des Hundes. Zbl. Phsyiol.*, 21 (1907).

Nalyor, L. E., *Poodles*, Williams & Norgate Ltd., 1954.

Pearson, K., and Usher, C. H., "Albinism in Dogs." *Biometrica*, 21:144-163 (1929).

Razran, H. S., and Warden, C. J., "The Sensory Capacities of the Dog (Russian Schools)." *Psychol. Bulletin* 26, 1929.

Stetson, J., "Heartworm Can Be Controlled." *Field and Stream* (June 1954).

Telever, J., 1934. When is the Heat Period of the Dog?

Wagner, John P., *The Boxer*, New York, Orange Judd Pub. Co., 1950.

Whitney, L. F., *The Basis of Breeding*. N. H. Fowler, 1928.

———— *How To Breed Dogs*. New York, Orange Judd Pub. Co., 1947.

———— *Feeding Our Dogs*, D. van Nostrand Co., Inc. New York, 1949.

———— and Whitney, G. D., *The Distemper Complex*. Practical Science Pub. Co., 1953.

INDEX

254